15.45
8A

The Winning Family

Choose the way of life.
Choose the way of love.
Choose the way of caring.
Choose the way of hope.
Choose the way of belief in tomorrow.
Choose the way of trusting.
Choose the way of goodness.
It's up to you. It's your choice.

—Leo F. Buscaglia[1]

The Winning Family

Increasing Self-Esteem in Your Children and Yourself

Dr. Louise Hart

Illustrated by
Kristen Baumgardner

Dodd, Mead & Company
New York

*To my children; Damian, Kristen, and Felix Baumgardner,
with gratitude and love. They have been my best cheerleaders.*

1   2   3   4   5   6   7   8   9   10

Library of Congress Cataloging-in-Publication Data

Hart, Louise.

The winning family.

*Bibliography: p.
Includes index.
1. Self-respect.   2. Self-respect in children.
3. Child rearing.   I. Title.*
BF697.5.S46H37   1987   649'.1'019   87-12146
ISBN 0-396-09182-2 {PBK.}
ISBN 0-396-09053-2

Contents

Contents

Acknowledgments

I gratefully acknowledge the encouragement and support for writing this book that I received from my family, friends, and teachers; the many parents who have shared their struggles, successes and insights; and Kathy May, who believed in me before I believed in myself.

My special thanks to Kate Fotopoulos, my wonderful editor and team member, for her dependability and her skill in helping me to put onto paper the concepts that are closest to my heart.

Introduction

I have written for you the book I wish had been available to me twenty years ago—and to my mother forty years ago, and to her mother before that. But we cannot turn back time. We must begin where we are now and move forward.

The biological parent-child connection is the deepest natural bond there is. It continues even after separation by death. From the moment they first appear, children introduce a totally new dimension into our lives that expands, challenges, deepens, sweetens, and at times exhausts us. Our children present us with ongoing opportunities to grow.

I write as a parent who has been there—stretching and growing in the process of my own life—and also as a community psychologist trying to prevent mental illness through teaching lifeskills for building healthier, happier individuals and families.

Like many people today, I have lived in a variety of family forms. When I was born, my mother ran the household while my father worked outside the home. I had the benefit of living in an extended family and had relatives other than my parents to look to as models. After college I got married, taught school for four years, and then was a full-time, stay-at-home mom in my nuclear family for thirteen years.

During that time my young family moved to Colorado. My mother, brothers, and sister lived a thousand miles east and west, so the family had little contact with grandparents, aunts, uncles, and cousins. We were relatively isolated until my husband's parents moved west and settled about thirty miles away from us.

At the time of this writing, my family has yet another form. After living for several years in a single-parent household, each of my three children is attending college, working, and discovering the world, while my lectures and workshops are taking me around the country and beyond. Now that we are living separately, we look forward with excitement to our reunions.

Familes come in many diverse forms and sizes, from large extended families to a "family of one," and they change over the course of a lifetime. Regardless of the living arrangements, deep connections will always link family members. This book can be helpful for any person, from any type of family, who wants to let go of dysfunctional patterns and reach for health, joy, and satisfaction—who believes that everyone can be a winner and no one has to lose.

A Winning Family begins with good intentions. Yet good intentions are not enough. We must reexamine what we know about raising children. *We need to learn from old mistakes rather than repeat them.* We need to be willing to examine and replace negative habits and patterns in our own lives.

And since we can't give what we don't have, we need to learn how to raise our own self-esteem along with our children's. Self-esteem is the greatest gift a parent can give to a child—certainly the most important! Parents can begin a positive program early in the lives of their children by laying a solid, loving foundation that builds self-esteem before the outside world has a major impact.

Parents can help *prevent low self-esteem*—and keep their loved ones from

- vulnerability to peer pressure
- dropping out of school
- eating disorders
- drug and alcohol abuse
- other addictive behaviors
- suicide

And parents can *promote high self-esteem* so that their children

- resist dependencies and addictions
- are enthusiastic about life (and school!)
- make friends easily
- trust themselves
- are self-directed
- are cooperative and follow reasonable rules
- are creative and imaginative
- take pride in their achievements
- are basically happy individuals
- are an asset to society and to the world!

With three children of my own, I have come to learn that parents have a great deal of influence and control over children's lives; we have control over family rules, communication styles, and family climate. Of course, there are areas in which we have little or no control. The cultural climate profoundly affects us all; we are cast into its mold. Yet at the same time, we also create it. Seen in this light, culture can limit or expand us, entrap or enhance us. If we clearly identify dangers, we can empower our children to cope with problems and challenges, to make choices instead of being victims.

The Winning Family delves into commonly encountered problems and offers healthy solutions. It teaches new skills to effectively meet the challenges of living with and raising kids in a complex world.

There is no one right way to parent; there are many. And you need to find the way that works for you. Become an expert on your family—you know them better than anyone else. Learn to trust yourself. Learn to take good care of yourself, for your own sake and for theirs.

Parenting can be a loving and enjoyable experience. If it's not, look for new skills, new methods, and new strategies that will be effective in *your* situation. And as a tennis pro once said, "If your game's not working, change it."

I support you and wish you the best.

Chapter One

You Are Building a Cathedral

*"Our children give us the opportunity to become the parents
we always wished we'd had."*
—L. Hart[1]

Many years ago, two men were working at the same job on the outskirts of a European city. A stranger approached them and asked, "What are you doing?" The first man replied with an edge of resentment, "I'm hauling rocks." The second man, when asked the same question, enthusiastically replied, "I'm building a cathedral!"

Just as skilled craftsmen designed cathedrals to be inspiring, to stand tall and strong, and to resist the elements over the years, we who raise and teach and care for children are working to build in them the strength and skills to live happy, creative, productive lives. This vitally important work is too often undervalued and unsupported.

We are the products of our families, our culture, and our time—and of these three, family has the strongest influence. My parents gave me more than they ever received. They had had difficult times as children in Germany. The first of twelve children, my mother grew up with adult responsibilities. Her mother had died delivering the fourth baby, and her father's new wife continued to have and raise children.

The primary focus in that family was survival; the primary value was work. And my parents transmitted those values to us. With the best of intentions, they did all they could for their children. But they couldn't give what they didn't have. "How can I love when I never was loved?" my mother asked.

Many people operate under the assumption that since parenting is a natural function of adult human beings, we should instinctively know how to do it—and do it well. The truth is, effective parenting requires study and practice like any other skilled profession. Who would even consider turning an untrained surgeon loose in an operating room? Yet we "operate" on our children every day.

Things just weren't right for me as a child. I was confused, lost, and lonely. I felt unloved. I had no self-esteem—I had no self. When I was pregnant with my first child in the early 1960s, I made a very important decision, probably the most important decision of my life. I made a commitment: *to raise my children the way I would like to have been raised*. This was not easy to do since I had no models. I became (as did other parents around me) a pioneer. After examining and reexamining everything I knew about parenting, I gave my kids what I thought was best.

My children, now young adults, are basically healthy, happy, responsible individuals with good self-esteem. What continues to delight me is that I receive from them what I have given: acceptance, respect, love, and support. Children deserve the best, and over time what goes around, comes around.

As children, we had no choice about how we were parented. Now, however, we do have choices. We can pass on, without questioning, what we experienced—or we can choose to raise our own children differently.

Unless you happen to have studied developmental psychology and family systems, you probably learned how to parent from *your* parents. For better or worse, you were taught by the examples they set: what they were is what you learned. If you felt loved and valued as a child and if you've become a competent, healthy adult, you were fortunate to have had good modeling. Raising kids should be relatively easy for you. But if you do not like the way you were raised—if you were rejected, neglected, or abused in any way, if you grew up in an alcoholic or other dysfunctional family system—you can choose differently. *You can rise above old, destructive patterns* to create a healthy life for yourself and your family.

You will need to question, sift, and sort through old "tapes," habits, and patterns. *Pass on the best—and throw away the rest.* This commitment is your best assurance that whatever negative patterns you may have grown up with will not be repeated in your children's generation.

Today we are becoming more and more aware of the impact our choices have on our children's future. We can choose to look back at our childhoods, identify the consequences of various parenting strategies, and sort them into "growthful" or "harmful." Then we can consciously pick the ones we want to hand down to our own children.

Both negative and positive experiences contribute to our parenting skills. It's like the Twenty Questions game: a no is every bit as valuable as a yes because it helps us narrow the field of options. If we insist on idealizing the past, denying any pain or suffering we may have experienced, we run the risk of unconsciously repeating painful behaviors with our children—even if we swore we never would. We have all felt wounded at times. Instead of wounding our own children, let's use our love for them as an inspiration to heal ourselves.

● Give your children what you want back. If you respect and accept them, they will learn to respect and accept; if you abuse and reject them, they will learn to abuse and reject. It's like a hug; you have to give one away if you want to get one back. Children are natural imitators. They reflect how you think, how you love, what you value, how you solve problems, what you do with feelings, and how you are in the world. You are teaching self-esteem, whether you know it or not. So be your best self, and they will want to become their best, too.

Parenting gives you an opportunity to create joy and love. It also encourages you to develop desirable personal qualities (such as patience), to understand and appreciate *yourself* at deeper levels, and to learn new skills. Your children become your best teachers.

One mother, Anne, said, "My lessons began with bonding. As I held my beautiful baby, I experienced a totally unconditional love between us, and a wonderful sense of euphoria. I was aware and appreciative of my uniqueness. My twenty-two-month-old son has taught me so many lessons. He's taught me what love is, he's taught me self-acceptance, and he's taught me to relax and let him go through his stages."

Our children are inheriting a complex, challenging world and need to be adequately prepared for it. As parents and other caring adults we can help them to become healthy, responsible people equipped with the skills to solve the problems of tomorrow.

Chapter Two

About Self-Esteem

*"What a man thinks of himself, that it is which determines
or rather indicates his fate."*
—Henry David Thoreau[1]

● Self-esteem is the greatest gift you can give your child—and yourself.
It is the key to mental health, learning, and happiness. It is knowing
that you are worthwhile and lovable.

Self-esteem evolves through the quality of the relationships between
children and those who are important in their lives. Children can't see
themselves directly. They can see only how others react and respond
to them: whether they are taken seriously and listened to, whether they
are respected and enjoyed. *Children observe, then draw conclusions.*
Their conclusions become their truth, their basic beliefs about who
they are and what they deserve in life. Sometimes their conclusions
are faulty; their truth is not true—merely one way of looking at things.

Children often view parents and authority figures as all-knowing and
all-powerful. They think *Those important people treat me as I deserve
to be treated. What they say about me is what I am.* When children
are respected, they conclude that they *deserve* respect; they develop
self-respect. When they are treated with esteem, when they are cher-
ished, they conclude that they *deserve* esteem, and they develop
self-esteem. On the other hand, if they are mistreated or abused, they
conclude that they deserve *that*—that they had it coming.

The truth is, no one deserves abuse or harmful punishment. Every
single child—every single person—deserves respect, acceptance, and
unconditional love.

Parents are, in effect, like mirrors. The reflection they give becomes
the basis for their children's self-image, influencing all aspects of their
lives.

Children learn from words, attitudes, and nonverbal messages from
the important people in their lives. Adults learn the same way: by observing and concluding. But it is easier to develop positive self-esteem
at the outset than to try to repair damaged self-esteem later. Yet we
cannot turn back the clock. We must start where we are now. If your

5

children are older, it's not too late: a new approach, new skills, and a dash of forgiveness can begin the healing process.

A thirty-five-year-old woman told me that she barely spoke to her mother from the time she was about eight or nine until she was twenty-six and divorcing from her first husband. Only then did they begin to share feelings, to develop a sense of trust in each other, to work through some of the misunderstandings and unintentional hurts that had come between them. Today they have a warm, supportive, and loving relationship.

It's obviously easier to develop self-esteem if you know how to go about it. Good intentions start you on the right path. Information and application (putting the ideas into practice) move you closer to your goal. As little as five minutes a day trying out new strategies with your children can produce positive changes.

So what do you do first? Self-esteem begins with self-love, with respecting, accepting, and taking care of *yourself*. That love spills over to your children, who learn to love themselves and to love you. Karl Menninger once said that love cures people—those who give it and those who receive it.

Self-esteem also depends on *unconditional* love: love with no strings attached; love with respect, acceptance, empathy, sensitivity, and warmth; love that says, "Regardless of what you do, I love and accept you for who you are. (See Chapter 18.)

A day-care provider told me about two-and-a-half-year-old Joey, who would say when he got in trouble, "That's okay, because my mom and dad still love me!" His parents had laid a solid, loving foundation.

Conditional love, on the other hand, is turned on and off. It manipulates behavior by saying, "I love you *when, because,* or *if* you do something." Kids who receive only conditional love never really *feel* loved; if they receive it they can't trust it. These kids try to *earn* love, by becoming people pleasers.

Children have their own life force, their own opinions, dreams, destinies. The task of parents is to allow and encourage children to be themselves while guiding, supporting, and celebrating their process of growth. Successful parenting involves not only unconditional love, but also the protection, limit setting, and responsibility appropriate to the child's developmental stage. Newborn infants are totally dependent on adults for their well-being, but growing children need the freedom to *be* and *act* their age. It's important to turn over responsibility to children as they are ready. If you're helping your kid across the street at three, that's great, but if he or she is fifteen, you have a problem. Let your children be silly, let them play, let them be kids while they're kids. When you understand the character of children at different ages, it makes it easier for you to work *with* their nature, not *against* it.

The letting-go process is a gradual, orderly transfer of freedom and responsibility from parent to child, from birth to maturity. Through this process, children gain self-confidence, independence, and self-esteem. By the time they are young adults, they will be responsible individuals equipped with the lifeskills they need to function happily and effectively.

Pause for a moment to reflect on your own self-esteem, as a child and as an adult. Over the years you have had your ups and downs. What were the causes? Take a few minutes to write down the things that have affected your self-esteem.

Low self-esteem comes from

- rejection
- conditional love or no love at all
- threats
- lack of attention, being ignored
- emotional or physical neglect
- abusive touch
- comparison, perfectionism, always looking for what's wrong
- not being taken seriously, not being listened to
- put-downs, name-calling, ridicule, humiliation, judgment, criticism, discouragement
- disrespect
- prejudice
- resentment
- needs not being met
- stress
- focusing on externals (appearances, behavior, performance)

Remember that when children experience this kind of treatment, they conclude, "I'm not important." "I can't do things right." "I'm not good enough." "I'm not okay." This becomes their Truth, and their self-esteem plunges.

On the other hand, high self-esteem comes from

- attention
- acceptance, respect, love
- honesty
- affectionate and appropriate touch
- having needs taken seriously and met
- honoring uniqueness

- having choices
- looking for what's right and positive
- encouragement, support, appreciation
- high and reasonable expectations; believing in your kids
- being really listened to and understood
- safety
- a sense of personal power
- a sense of connection with a Higher Power (spirituality)
- a feeling of connectedness with others
- being responsible
- having meaning in life, a sense of purpose
- being healthy and fit
- forgiveness and gratitude
- play

As children observe and experience these positive influences in their lives, they conclude, "I'm okay." "I'm glad to be me." "Mom and Dad think I'm important; I must matter." "I'm worthwhile." "I'm loved." Their self-esteem soars. If you stop doing these things that lower self-esteem and do more and more of the things that raise self-esteem, you will notice marked improvements in your family relations. Over time, low self-esteem can be healed.

I recently realized that when I'm behaving from the low self-esteem mode, my kids feel bad, *and so do I*. On the other hand, when I'm operating from high self-esteem, everyone's self-esteem increases! When I'm good to them, we all come out winning, and when I'm nasty, we suffer. For better or worse, self-esteem is contagious.

We make butterflies by feeding caterpillars, not by trying to paste wings on them. Kids need to like themselves the way they are, and we can help them develop a positive self-image.

Self-Esteem Building Exercise

Get a partner to do this with you. Sit facing each other. One person, A, looks the other, B, in the eyes and says, "Tell me how you're terrific!" That's the only thing that A says.

B responds by saying, "I'm terrific because . . ." and completes the sentence. B repeats this sentence with different endings for three or four minutes. At the end of this time you switch roles.

After you both have taken a turn, talk about it. How was it to hear those terrific things about your partner? How was it to say those terrific things about yourself?

Many people get embarrassed because they haven't thought of themselves in terms of terrific-ness. Many feel as if they're bragging. Yet Will Rogers said, "If it's the truth, it can't be bragging." "Flip" your focus from negative to positive.

Helen, a grandmother attending a workshop, shared her awareness after the exercise: "I got in touch with my roots—with who I really am. I went back to the joy of the little girl I used to be—before I was contaminated with the negative messages of growing up."

Start catching yourself—and your kids—being terrific. You *are* terrific—and so are they. Look for all the good you have at home. *Whatever you look for, you find.*

Self-Esteem Protection Skills

"No one can make you feel inferior without your consent."
—Eleanor Roosevelt[2]

Negative social influences challenge your self-esteem. When people offer you a helping of their "garbage," can you say, "No, thank you," and go on with your business, or do you let them threaten your self-esteem? Kids are frequently yelled at, teased, put down, and compared, and their self-esteem sags.

Everyone needs strategies for protecting and enhancing self-esteem. The better you feel about yourself, the less vulnerable you will be to external circumstances. With high self-esteem, you know that you don't have to put up with put-downs. Here are some strategies for dealing with negative barbs and arrows:

- **Separate yourself from the other person's behavior.** Often others are acting *for* themselves, and not *against* you.
- **Consider the source.** Some people seem to wallow in negativity. Let them express whatever emotions they choose and know that you have little or nothing to do with their feelings.
- **Inquire.** Asking, "What do you mean by that?" throws the responsibility for the statement back on them and invites them to talk about it.
- **Explore.** Ask them, "Is something wrong?"
- **Confront.** Ask them, "Do you think that ———?" "In what way am I ———?" Again, these questions make the other person take responsibility.
- **Disagree.** You might say, "I understand that you feel that way, but I disagree."

- **Don't take it personally.** Maybe they're having a bad day; the nastiness probably has nothing to do with you.
- **Blend.** Figure out what they're feeling and reflect it back. "Sounds like you're feeling angry." Empathic listening will probably dissipate/calm/reduce their anger. (See Chapter 4.)
- **Make a neutral remark.** When they finish, say, "Oh," or, "I see."
- **Give feedback.** If it hurts, you might say, "Ouch—that hurts!" Then ask if they meant to hurt you.
- **Use positive self-talk.** Repeat over and over to yourself, "No matter what you say or do to me, I'm still a worthwhile person."[3] Teach this to your kids and to anyone who is in a toxic or abusive situation.
- **Withdraw.** Some people choose to get away from that person.

Here are strategies that have worked for other people:

- **"Wax your back."** A dear friend of mine told me that every morning he waxes his back and his life is great. No, it isn't to rid himself of superfluous hair; it's to protect him from whatever negativity might "rain" on him in the business world, just as oily feathers protect a duck. He takes preventive measures to safeguard his self-esteem.
- **Humor.** Some people make a joke out of unpleasant situations.
- **Clothing and jewelry.** Wonder Woman had bracelets and a "golden girdle." People wear "power" clothes when they want to make a powerful impression—when, for example, they want to borrow money from a bank.
- **Permission to be different.** Kids often get a lot of pressure to be like everyone else. They get teased because they are wearing the wrong kind of jeans, for example. If you teach them that they are unique and don't have to act and dress like everyone else, they'll be less affected by those pressures. Give them permission to be different—to be who they really are.

Try these strategies, or some of your own, until you find one that works for you, that helps you deal with negativity without damaging your self-esteem.

Chapter Three

"I know they love me, but I don't feel it."

"The remarkable thing is that we really love our neighbor as ourselves: we do unto others as we do unto ourselves. We hate others when we hate ourselves. We are tolerant toward others when we tolerate ourselves. We forgive others when we forgive ourselves. It is not love of self but hatred of self which is at the root of the troubles that afflict our world."

—Eric Hoffer[1]

In my workshops I ask parents how many *knew* while growing up that they were loved by their parents. Many hands usually go up. Then I ask how many *felt* loved; fewer hands are raised.

Sometimes parents who really love their children don't know how to convey that love; sometimes the children don't know how to accept it. A parent of a teenage bulimic confessed, "My daughter never felt loved, but I loved her very much!" Being loved does not necessarily mean feeling loved.

In our society, many men were taught from childhood not to feel. Having learned to block out difficult feelings, they unfortunately also blocked out the beautiful feeling of love. Shere Hite's survey of seven-thousand men revealed that almost none of them were close to their fathers. Raising children was often considered "woman's work," and fathers working away from home for long hours had little contact with their kids. One survey revealed that fathers spent an average of thirty-seven seconds a day interacting with their infants. Another showed a marked decrease in contact after a divorce: by early adolescence, 50 percent of the children from divorced families had *no* contact with their dads, 30 percent had *sporadic* contact, and only 20 percent saw their fathers *once a week* or more.[2] Yet children need their dads as well as their moms. They need to feel loved by them. And dads need to love and feel loved by their children.

If you did not learn to love as a child, now is the time. Learn to give love, to receive love, to love yourself. Then you can nurture, love, and parent your children.

> *"If we cannot love ourselves,*
> *where will we draw our love for anyone else?"*
> —Newman and Berkowitz[3]

I choose to believe that most parents probably did love their children, but because of personal shortcomings and miscommunications, the children did not feel loved. Their self-esteem suffered needlessly.

I recently heard about a couple celebrating their twenty-fifth wedding anniversary. The wife told her husband that she had been showing her love all those years by warming his plates for him. He replied, "I hate having warm plates!" Apparently they then were able to work through this miscommunication because they went on to celebrate their thirtieth anniversary—probably with cold plates.

What Does *Not* Communicate Love

Parents with good intentions try to show their love in many ways that don't work, such as:

• **Overpermissiveness.** Parents think, "My kids know that I love them because I let them do anything they want." A high school friend of mine who could stay out as late as she wanted came to the conclusion that her parents didn't care enough to set a curfew. Children need safe, healthy, and reasonable limits; our willingness to set these limits conveys love.

• **Martyrdom.** Many women were taught to be self-sacrificing—continually giving to others without taking care of themselves. They set aside their own needs, believing that was the way to express love for their families. Many ended up as martyrs and doormats. By putting themselves last, they came to feel resentful and depleted, and their children did not feel loved. These parents did too much for their children—things that the children should have been doing for themselves (including solving problems), which deprived the children of the opportunity to learn, gain confidence, and build their self-esteem. These children came to expect that someone else would always "do it for them." It is important for parents to take care of themselves, to see to their own needs. Then they will have more to give to those they love.

• **Overprotection.** In this sometimes scary world we live in, our children need to be protected from danger and harm. However, if we overprotect them, they conclude that they aren't capable—not that they are loved.

• **Quantity time without quality.** Spending lots of time together does not necessarily communicate love. Parents may spend all day with their children yet never really be there for them. The *quality* of time spent together is more important than the quantity. Many people raised by adults who were with them twenty-four hours a day felt unloved.

• **Material possessions.** Linda, a thirty-six-year-old mom, told me, "My father would buy me anything I wanted, but he would never hug me or show me any affection. I've spent my whole life feeling that he didn't love me." Material things may be a substitute for love; in themselves, they do not convey love. The best thing to spend on your children is time.

What *Does* Communicate Love

Larry, an older man in my workshop, said, "I felt loved when my dad carried me on his shoulders and sang to me." One woman felt loved when the family built an ice rink and then went skating together. The love in their families increased, as did the self-esteem. It was great fun that created those endearing memories.

Take a few moments and ask yourself what situations made you feel loved as a child. Are you doing things like that for or with your children?

There are many ways we can communicate love effectively to children, including:

• **Taking them seriously.** The things that happen in your children's lives are of tremendous importance to them. Put yourself in their shoes and value what they share with you.

• **Really listening.** This is one of the most basic and important lifeskills and will be taught in the next chapter.

• **Being with, not doing for.** It's easy to get caught up in always doing things *for* children. Yet it's important, at times, to put aside all the busyness and just *be* there with them. This is especially true in times of crisis. When children (and others) feel this quality of presence, they conclude, "It's important for you to be with me. I must matter. I am loved." Their self-esteem goes up—and so does yours.

How can we communicate to children that they are worthwhile and valuable?

- **Non-verbal messages.** Positive facial expressions, eye contact, loving touch, and attentiveness make others feel important.
- **Positive words.** Everyone wants to hear good things about themselves. Make sure your words are sincere.
- **Respect and enjoyment.** Children read our attitudes. When we have fun with them, everybody wins.

"If everyone had just one single person in his life to say, 'I will love you no matter what. I will love you if you are stupid, if you slip and fall on your face, if you do the wrong thing, if you make mistakes, if you behave like a human being—I will love you no matter,' then we'd never end up in mental institutions."

—Leo F. Buscaglia[4]

Chapter Four

Effective Communication: Listening Skills

"To the depth that I am willing to reveal myself to you,
to that depth can I know myself."
—John Powell[1]

Kids who grew up under the "children should be seen and not heard" belief had a distinct handicap. They were deprived of the opportunity to express their thoughts and opinions and to gain confidence in their abilities. Many of them came to believe that what they had to say wasn't important, that they weren't important, or even that no one cared about them. Their self-esteem suffered.

The first time I felt really listened to, I was about seventeen years old. I spent the night at my friend Annie's home. She and I talked and talked into the early morning. Annie cared about what I had to say and really listened to me! I felt surprise, relief, joy, and closeness. Really listening expresses interest and caring. It is a powerful and intimate experience that enhances self-esteem and friendship.

Remember a time when you had something very important to say but the person you were talking to was *not* listening well; the listener either wasn't interested, or didn't know how to listen, or perhaps it was just a bad time to bring up that particular subject. What was that like for you? What did you feel?

Some people feel rejected, angry, unimportant, worthless, or unloved when they're not heard; they may want to close off or withdraw. Carl Jung once said that people are in institutions because no one would listen to their stories.

Communication skills are the most basic, important skills that we need in life. Without them we are doomed to continual frustration, misunderstandings, and loneliness. Ever since the intrusion of television into family time—when people sit back passively and ignore each other—communication patterns have changed dramatically, and many vital skills have been lost. Wendy Sarkissian, an Australian social planner who conducted extensive research in the suburbs of New South Wales, stated, "My view is that whole generations of women are being lost to us. . . . I've talked to women who've lived for four and a half years across the street from other women and have never even introduced themselves because they seem to have lost the skills of getting to know people, the skills of operating comfortably with other women or with other people."[2] With communication skills we can develop friendships and deep love relationships that enrich our lives and enhance our families.

I once spoke with a Hmong from a hill tribe in Laos about his life. The villagers there live simple lives without telephones, electricity, or any of the forms of entertainment to which I am accustomed. I asked him what they do during the long monsoon season. He responded, "We tell stories!" Everyone in that culture naturally learns to tell stories and to listen well. Having no written language, the transmission of their cultural history depends on the people's communication skills.

In our culture, few people are taught to listen, yet active listening skills aren't difficult to learn. Once you learn to use them and teach them to others, they will transform your relationships and raise self-esteem.

- *Be interested. Look interested.* Look into the eyes of the speaker. (When listening to children, sit or crouch down to be at their eye level.) Face the speaker directly; if you are both sitting, lean forward slightly.
- *Put aside judgment and criticism.* Get into their experience and feelings; get inside their shoes and try to understand what happened. Put yourself and your own concerns aside; don't be thinking about what you'll say next.
- *Be aware of nonverbal cues.* Note the speed and inflection of the voice; the sighs and gulps; posture; the eyes glazing over or tearing. Reading between the lines gives you important information.
- *Let them finish.* Don't interrupt. While you are the listener, let the speaker do the talking. At times if may be okay to briefly interject something *if* it enhances the other's story. The speaker has the ball; do not take it away. This may be difficult for those who are used to communicating competitively—impatiently

waiting for a comma, then jumping in. Put your total attention on the speaker. You'll get your turn afterward.

If you have actively listened, you have gathered much information. You noticed body language; you probably figured out the feelings involved—you know what you would have felt if this had happened to you.

- *Reflect these feeling(s)* back to the other person, from his or her point of view. For example, "I bet you were scared," or "You must have been really excited," or "You must feel _____ because _____."[3]

If you have listened and reflected accurately, the speaker will probably breathe a sigh of relief at being understood or perhaps will exclaim excitedly, "Yes, that's right!" If you have not reflected accurately, the speaker has an opportunity to clear the misunderstanding. Once this is completed, the conversation can take one of several turns. The listener can help the speaker explore the situation ("Would you do it that way again?") or offer guidance ("I don't think that was a good idea"). Then the listener can speak, expanding upon that topic or dealing with another issue.

Practice active listening with someone. Find a time that is convenient for both. Read this section together, then take turns being the speaker and the listener, each talking for about two or three minutes. Afterward, discuss how it felt. Did you really feel listened to? If not, what might your partner have done differently so that you would feel listened to? Give feedback in a positive way; for example, "When I noticed your arms were folded, I thought you weren't interested in what I had to say. I would appreciate it if you didn't fold your arms when you listen to me."

If, as the speaker, you were really listened to, you probably experienced some or all of these feelings: excitement, interest, a sense of closeness to the listener, validation, worth, understanding, love. As a listener you probably felt interest, trust, enrichment from a new experience, excitement, and closeness to the speaker. Self-esteem on both sides has increased. This is *win-win communication.*

Think back to the time when you felt you weren't being heard. Who came out winning? No one.

Active listening skills need to be practiced. At first they may feel awkward and artificial. That's okay; keep at it, and they'll get easier. After a while they will be automatic.

Good listeners take the time to listen. They help people discover that they have stories to tell. Good listening keeps people healthy and happy. It's an important skill that can improve the quality of your family life, your relationships, and everyone's self-esteem.

"If you take time to talk together each day, you'll never become strangers."
—Leo F. Buscaglia[4]

Chapter 5

Asking and Refusal Skills

"So much to say. And so much not to say! Some things are better left unsaid.
But so many unsaid things can become a burden."
—Virginia Mae Axline[1]

Communication skills have two parts: listening skills and sending (or speaking) skills. Listening skills are essential for understanding, for resolving differences, for closeness, and for love. Sending skills are essential for letting others know what we want and don't want and for getting needs met. In teaching children to ride a bicycle, we teach them how to control it: how to make it go and stop, how to turn. Sending skills are as basic; they help us stop what we don't want and turn toward what we do want—they give us control over our lives.

There are three basic ways to get what we want: monster ways, mouse ways, and assertive ways.

Monster ways include shouting, getting angry, hitting, manipulating, and intimidating others. *Mouse ways* include crying, whining, begging, pouting, hinting, and hoping someone will read your mind. ("If he really loves me, he'll know what I want!" This works only if he is psychic.) Monster and mouse communication styles may work, but they usually create bad feelings in the process.[2]

The best way to communicate is by *assertive ways*. They involve knowing what you want and then asking or telling others: "Would you help me?" "I'd really like to get together more often." "I don't like it when you. . . ." "Please give me a hug." When we ask for what we want, we are much more likely to get it, remembering, of course, that it is important to be sensitive to the timing of the question/request.

It's okay to ask for what you want. Asking is not a sign of weakness or failure, but a tool for helping you get your needs met. It may feel strange at first, but it will get easier. It's also okay to *get* what you want—and to let people help you.

19

We can ask questions to express interest and caring for others. Open-ended questions ("Would you tell me about your day?") encourage more talking than questions that can be answered with one word or a phrase ("How are you?" "Fine.") To improve communication, ask, "What do you feel?" "What do you want?" "How can I help?" Asking, in a respectful tone of voice, can lead to greater understanding.

Teaching children to ask empowers them to get their needs met. Young children who know how to ask for a glass of water, for example, don't have to whine or cry or act out in other undesirable ways to get their thirst quenched.

Everyone also needs to be able to say no. As adults, no lets us set limits for our children and ourselves. It helps us maintain integrity. Children also need to be able to say no. Sadly, the media are filled with stories of children being manipulated in unhealthy ways. As youngsters, children need to learn that their bodies belong to them alone and that they have the right to say no to anyone who might try to touch them. We need to teach older children to say no to drugs and alcohol. If they have not been taught refusal skills, children will be vulnerable to pressure and manipulation, to pitfalls and dangers.

Many people have great difficulty saying no. If this is a problem for you, complete this sentence several times: "Saying no means _____."

Allow yourself to become aware of why it is difficult for you to say no.

One of the reasons people have difficulty saying no is that they have negative associations with the word. Perhaps you find this true of yourself. For many people, saying no means rejection, selfishness, guilt, failure, weakness, stubbornness, hurting others' feelings, not being liked by others, risking anger. No wonder they have such difficulties!

I invite you to now think of the *value* of saying no. Write your thoughts down before reading further.

Saying no is like giving yourself a present—of honesty, freedom (you don't feel used), relief, authority, peace, power, confidence, and integrity. It establishes boundaries. It gives you self-definition and self-respect. It gives you time and control over your own life.

As parents we must say no when our children's health or safety is at risk. Like anything else, however, *no* can be overused, rendering it ineffective (like the boy who cried wolf). Say no to your children with respect and firmness; a smile may confuse them. Avoid being nasty: you don't have to be mean to mean business.

Last summer, for example, my eighteen-year-old told me he wanted to go sky-diving with his friends. I laughed (probably out of nervousness); then I joked about it ("Well, Felix, do you have insurance?"). Then I firmly said, "No, you may not do it. I love you and want to enjoy you for many more years to come." He and his buddies went to the airport to watch what was going on, and after seeing the setup, he realized that he didn't even want to do it.

"It is not okay to say no if it is a responsibility or something you have agreed to do," writes Dr. Patricia Palmer. "And remember, how you say no makes a difference. Treat others as you like to be treated."

Women face additional difficulty in saying no because of the myth that "when she says no she really means yes." When women muster the courage to say no, the other person often does not take them seriously and thereby disempowers them. Certainly many cases of date-rape have resulted from this communication tangle. If saying no is hard for you, consider going to a therapist who can help you learn how.

People who talk and listen to others can form and maintain healthy, happy relationships. They can share ideas, opinions, and feelings without fearing judgment and criticism. Learning and practicing communication skills increases understanding, trust, openness, closeness, and love between people—and everyone's self-esteem goes up.

Chapter Six

Dealing with Feelings

*"It is terribly amusing how many different climates of feeling
I can go through in one day."*
—Anne Morrow Lindbergh[1]

High self-esteem is a positive feeling based on self-acceptance, self-respect, and self-love. It is accompanied by feelings of specialness, worthwhileness, appreciation, safety, personal power, belonging, and gratitude. If we are out of touch with our emotions, we cannot experience any of these feelings, nor can we have a positive sense of self-esteem.

Children are unique individuals, and it is important to respect and allow their separateness. They have different bodies, different minds, different dreams, and different feelings. "Your way of seeing and feeling is not the only way of seeing and feeling," writes Dorothy Corkille Briggs.

By accepting children's emotions—whatever they may be—you help them to "own" their feelings and to conclude, "My feelings are okay even when they're not the same as my dad's," "It's okay to be me," "I'm okay." And self-esteem goes up.

If you share your feelings, children (and spouses and friends) understand you more easily and don't have to rely on guessing what's happening with you. Talking things out releases internal pressures, helps you get some perspective, and opens you for support and caring. Not talking about feelings can create anxiety, tension, and distance. Whether you realize it or not, you teach your children how to handle *their* feelings by how you handle *yours*.

Feelings are private, internal experiences that tell us about our world. When we expect children to feel the way we do, we disrespect them and deny them their integrity. When we dictate how they should or shouldn't feel, we are pressuring them to give up their own emotional reality. They cannot do this; they cannot manufacture emotions.

They will only repress their true feelings and pretend to feel different.[2]

It's easy to try to force our feelings on others: "Say you're sorry!" "Tell me you love me." "You should be happy." "Don't be mad." Hearing these you-shouldn't-feel-how-you-feel messages, kids conclude that their feelings are unacceptable, wrong, or even nonexistent. They learn to stop sharing their feelings because they can't trust people with them. Not knowing what to do with their feelings, children hide them—from themselves and others—or deny them altogether. They become isolated in fear, worry, embarrassment, anger, or guilt. They start building protective walls around themselves that only serve to increase their isolation.

"Safety disappears," writes Briggs, "when you decide what children 'should' enjoy"—or feel. "Respect for separateness proves you care." Everyone has a right to his or her own feelings. And this right must be accepted and protected.

There is a Zen story about two monks whose vows forbade them to look upon or speak with women. One day they were walking by a stream when they came upon a woman carrying an awkward, heavy load. The first monk, terribly flustered, pulled his hood up over his head and turned quickly away. The second, seeing the woman's distress, picked her up with her bundles and carried her across the stream. All the way back to the monastery the first monk chided the second, "How could you possibly have done that? Don't you realize you've broken your holy vows?" After listening to that harangue for over an hour, the second monk finally said, "Brother, I carried the woman across the stream, but you have carried her for five miles!"

We have complete choice as to how to respond to any situation in our lives. Our attitude determines whether or not we will let external circumstances bring us down. (See Chapter 4.)

Feelings are directly connected to thoughts (or self-talk), and also to behavior.

THOUGHTS→FEELINGS→BEHAVIOR

Negative thoughts lead to negative feelings, which lead to negative behavior. On the other hand, positive thoughts lead to positive feelings and positive behavior. (See Chapter 16.)

For example, a child thinks about an ice cream cone, which creates a feeling (desire for a double-dip chocolate chip cone), which leads to behavior (doing something to get a cone).

In dealing with this situation, you could decide to buy a cone or not. If you choose not to buy one, it is very easy to slip into denial of your child's feelings. ("You don't really want a cone right now"), or to manipulate his or her feelings ("You shouldn't feel that way before dinner"). Instead, accept and acknowledge his or her feelings ("You'd sure like to get a cone right now"), then intervene at the thought level ("But it's too close to dinnertime and would probably spoil your appetite") or at the behavior level ("We can't get you one right now, honey").

Some people handle negative feelings by shouting, hitting, or using other aggressive, monster behaviors. This means of "expression" may give an illusion of release, but it actually damages the other person, the relationship, and everyone's self-esteem.

When eight-year-old Andy hits his little sister, a parent might yell, "Stop that! Say you're sorry. Give her a big hug." Those orders ignore and deny Andy's feelings and demand hypocritical behavior; he's *not* sorry, and he doesn't feel like hugging her!

Instead, try this: Stop the behavior. ("You may not hit your sister!") Then realize that the behavior came from a feeling and a thought. He's hitting for a reason; he's probably angry. Accept his anger and help him *turn his feelings into words*. ("You're mad. What's going on?") Get into his shoes and understand what happened from his point of view. (Use active listening skills; See Chapter 4.) Expressing and accepting negative feelings release their negative power. *Talking it out prevents acting it out.*

Redirect the negative behavior into positive actions: "When you're angry, you can pound the pillows on your bed or hit the punching bag. You may not hit your sister." Andy concludes, "My feelings are okay. And I'm okay." He also learns that it's *not* okay to hit his sister. He learns limits and healthy ideas for dealing with his anger next time.

Feelings have a legitimate purpose. They are part of being human and must be accepted. "Feelings seem inappropriate only when they are not understood," states Claudia Black. All feelings are okay. What we do with our feelings—our behavior—can be judged as acceptable or unacceptable. Allow the emotions and deal with the behavior.

When children hurt themselves, encourage them to say, "Ouch." If it hurts badly, have them say, "Ouch!!!" It helps to release and heal the pain. Often people hurt others without realizing it. Teaching children to express pain helps them let others know how they feel. Then they can ask for what they want. (See Chapter 5.)

Repressing feelings creates tension in the body that will continue to increase in pressure until it it released. This pressure may be turned against the self—in the form of psychosomatic or psychological problems—or it may be directed against others in the family or in society.

In our culture, little boys have often been taught to repress their feelings. When a pet died or when they injured themselves, they were told,

"Boys don't cry." They learned that they had to deny or "gunnysack" their feelings.

Everyone has pain and discomfort at one time or another. What are we taught to do with it? Our cultural messages teach us very clearly to avoid pain at all costs; we are taught to distract ourselves, to drug ourselves, or to be "strong" and deny that there's anything wrong. Yet pain is nothing more than a messenger telling us we need to change something. When we ignore the message, nothing changes, and we get stuck in the pain—in the problem. What we need to do is pay attention to it, figure our what's going on, and make some changes.

A journal is a wonderful tool for dealing with strong emotions, for sorting through confusion, for releasing tension. As you clarify your feelings, you begin to identify patterns in your emotional process that will help you to change and grow. A journal can start you on the path to becoming your own best friend.

Pause for a moment to remember your childhood. What feelings were expressed? How? What did you do with the *other* feelings? Do you want your own children to have the same experience?

Trust

Kids need to be able to trust their parents; parents must be trustworthy. Trust develops when others are there for you. A child wonders: "Can I depend on being fed when hungry, on being comforted when hurt or frightened?" "Are my needs fulfilled?" "Is the world a friendly, safe place to be?" "Are the people helpful? Can I count on them?" The child concludes either, "I can trust," or, "I cannot trust."

In a brainstorming session, parents defined trust as an act of faith, belief in the other, confidence, predictability, absence of fear, feeling safe, the basis for intimacy. In order for trust to develop, children must feel safe. It is up to the parents to create a safe environment for their children. In creating safety, parents lay the foundation for trust and health. An unsafe environment is a breeding ground for neuroses.

"The single most important ingredient in a nurturing relationship—in any relationship—is honesty," states Black.[3] Dishonesty creates confusion and destroys trust. Kids learn from you: if you do not tell the truth, neither will they. Let's resurrect the old saying, "Honesty is the best policy." No one can trust, or be expected to trust, unless people openly and honestly talk about what's important and about their feelings. This doesn't mean, though, that you have to say absolutely everything that's on your mind.

One woman told me that everyone in her home was taught truthfulness. "My parents encouraged us to say anything we wanted. But we had to be careful *how* we said it." She learned early in life how to be truthful, sensitive, and tactful.

When a baby is born, parents often start playing roles. They become less of who they really are and more of who they think they're *supposed* to be. When parents aren't being genuine, children find it difficult to know them or trust them.

> "In a very serious way, this transformation is unfortunate because it so often results in parents forgetting they are still humans with human faults, persons with personal limitations, real persons with real feelings. Forgetting the reality of their own human-ness . . . , they frequently cease to be human.
> —T. Gordon[4]

The same holds true when parents maintain a facade—of being perfect, for example.

Other things that damage trust are fear, neglect, insensitivity, ridicule, humiliation, rejection, and abuse.

I used to think that trust was like being pregnant—it was all or nothing at all; there was no in-between. Then I learned differently. I discovered that we must figure out how far and in what situations we can trust others. And the parent-child relationship calls for the greatest possible amount of trust.

Let's examine the concept of trust and how it can break down in the process of a relationship.

TRUST	A belief that another is trustworthy; safety exists.
DISAPPOINTMENT	An expectation is not fulfilled. (Too high and impossible expectations, as found in perfectionists, precipitate disappointment.)
SUSPICION	After a series of disappointments, the belief in the other's trustworthiness is questioned.
DISTRUST	The belief changes to "I can't trust that person." A credibility gap results. People become more guarded in their speech; when listening, they wonder what is behind the words, what is being withheld.
DEFENSIVENESS	Anger may build at having one's integrity questioned and because of the alienation and pain. Blame may enter with each trying to exonerate him/herself by accusing the other of being at fault.
WITHDRAWAL AND ALIENATION	With increasing distrust, people often choose to avoid each other. If this is not possible, they distance themselves. Speech is limited to what's not really important. People pull back, believing the other will fake a response, manipulate, or exploit them. They become strangers to each other. Yet, they may "go through the motions" in public to conceal the pain from others.
HOSTILITY	The trust has broken down. Fear and polarization result.[5]

Yet, broken trust is not forever. It can begin to heal as behaviors improve. Faulty communication (with miscommunication and misunderstandings) can damage trust. For example, learning good communication skills can help to clear it up. A counselor or therapist may be needed to guide and support the behavioral changes needed for the relationship to heal.

Your children's trust can be built in a variety of ways:

- Meet their needs.
- Avoid unpleasant surprises.
- Don't make promises you won't keep.
- Let them know they can count on you.

- Spend comfortable, quality time together.
- Tell them when and where you are going and when you'll return.
- Prepare them in advance for big events in their lives so they know what to expect.[6]

Kids need to be able to trust their parents. And parents need to be able to trust their kids. This begins with a leap of faith on the part of the parents—a gift of respect, of believing in them. With this comes the expectation and encouragement for them to be their best. Wanting to live up to your expectations, the kids become trustworthy. For this reason, my son Damian says that we have an obligation to trust others, so that we can enable them to be trustworthy and encourage them to be their best. We need to focus on their strong points and build on them. We also need to learn to trust ourselves more and thereby model trustworthiness. Doing this we create an environment where safety and honesty, connectedness and love flourish. This is the first step towards creating a winning family.

> *"I think we may safely trust a good deal more than we do."*
> —Henry David Thoreau[7]

Guilt

Guilt is a problem for many people. Feeling guilty, their self-esteem suffers. Reframing guilt—or finding another way of looking at it—helps to understand it, accept ourselves more, and begin to release its negative grip.

Guilt has been defined as moral self-disapproval. There are two types of guilt: general and specific.[8]

General guilt refers to total self-condemnation. "I am a bad person." "I am worthless." "I am evil." It is condemnation of the whole person, not a specific act or behavior. It comes from having important people condemn us—not what we *did,* but who we *are.* It is very painful.

General guilt occurs in persons who do not yet have a self-defined set of values and moral standards but who have a "secondhand" value system from parents, significant others, their church. Wanting to do what they are "supposed" to do, yet failing, these external-locus-of-control people have low self-esteem. (See Chapter 19.)

Specific guilt refers to one specific reproachful action. "I did something which was unworthy of me. I violated *my* standards." This limited guilt is experienced by persons who have self-defined principles

29

by which they live. It is much less painful than general guilt. When the mistake is corrected and forgiven, the guilt is released. (See Chapter 17 on perfectionism.) Internal-locus-of-control people are more likely to experience specific guilt: "I acted in good faith, but I had an error of knowledge or judgment."

The way parents deal with children's behavior can greatly influence feelings of guilt. Often parents use certain words that create negative feelings and thereby manipulate the child's behavior; for example, "I'm disappointed in you.") Although they may get the behavioral change they seek, parents may inadvertently create psychological problems for their children as well.

One forty-eight-year-old woman stated, "I wasted my childhood tormented with guilt and fear. I tried so hard to be good, yet I always felt bad. I tried to second-guess my mom all the time so I could avoid being blamed and criticized. I was a good little girl who grew up to be a nice lady paralyzed by fear and guilt. If, driving down the street, I'd see a policeman, I'd feel an intense wave of anxiety even though I had done nothing wrong! It took me years to get rid of the shackles of guilt and fear."

Statements that influence behavior while manipulating feelings include

- "I'm ashamed of you."
- "Don't get hurt! Be careful! Don't fall!"
- "You have to _____ so that I don't worry about you."
- "I'm so disappointed in you."
- "I love you when you _____" "I love you if you _____"

Children who grow up hearing these messages tend to be insecure and scared, or they feel guilty about everything.

Many parents see an unacceptable behavior, and then they overgeneralize; they don't deal with the one specific thing that the kid did wrong, but they confuse the issue by saying, "*You* are a bad person." They may blow it out of proportion by saying, "I can't believe that you would have even thought to do that!" If the kid was doing his or her best and trying to be good, the parents' response can be baffling. Feeling confused and not quite understanding what went wrong, the child might become reluctant to do *anything* for fear of displeasing the parents. This type of paralysis can "freeze" a child's development; the child may come to distrust himself or herself and suffer intensely from guilt and low self-esteem.

It's okay for a child to feel bad about doing a bad thing. But the child should not end up feeling like an awful person. The desired outcome is saying, "I did a bad thing, but I'm still a good person," then fixing whatever is wrong, learning from the mistake, and not repeating it.

People who feel a *lot* of guilt probably suffer from generalized guilt. Here are some ways you can deal with it:

- Minimize it. Ask yourself, What one specific action is the cause of the guilt?
- Find the source. Who or what is judging your behavior?
- Separate yourself from that guilt source.
- Ask yourself, deep inside, what you believe, want, and choose for yourself.
- Correct the guilt-producing behavior.
- Forgive yourself and let it go.

Take some time to examine your values and standards. One way to do this is to make a list of the rules in your childhood home. Evaluate them. Which do you want to keep? Which might you want to change? Once you begin to develop an "intrinsic conscience" based on your own values, beliefs, and choices, you will be released from general guilt. When you do something that *you* believe to be wrong, you will suffer *specific* guilt or regret that will serve to make you accountable and lead you to better behavior next time.

Anger

"Don't hold onto anger, hurt, or pain.
They steal energy and keep you from love."
—Leo F. Buscaglia[9]

Anger is a normal feeling. It identifies a problem needing a solution. We must learn to accept it in ourselves and others (especially our children), and we must learn to express it in a "clean," nondamaging way. As we learn how to deal with anger, it is easier to accept—in ourselves and in others.

If the intensity of your anger is out of proportion to the situation, you need to call a time-out to focus on what you "triggered." Writing in a journal is a good tool for figuring things out. Once you unravel them, you defuse the trigger. One mother told her therapist that she "lost it" when her baby cried. Delving into this problem, they discovered that she had a belief that if her baby cried, it meant she was a "bad mother." Understanding this, she saw the error and changed her belief, her feelings, and her behavior.

Like other emotions, anger is usually short-lived. This is partly because it comes mixed with other feelings—fear, frustration, and love. Take, for example, the situation of a child getting lost in a store. Mother probably feels anger, fear, love, and relief when they are reunited; the common response, however, is to express anger to the child. A healthier and more honest response would be to talk about the anger, then about the fear, the love—and the relief.

Jack Canfield teaches this "Total Truth Process."[10]

1. Express the anger: "I'm angry that you wandered off."
2. Express the pain and fear: "I was afraid that something bad might happen to you that would hurt you."
3. Express the "I'm sorrys": "I'm sorry that I was taking so long looking at blouses."
4. Express the wants: "What I want is for you to stay close enough to see me so I know you're okay. I want you to be safe and content. Maybe if I brought along some books or toys it would be more fun for you."
5. Express love, forgiveness, appreciation: "I am so glad that you are okay! I love you so much and don't want anything bad to happen to you." Hug and comfort the frightened child.

Many people get "stuck" in the anger, the pain, or the fear. Express one feeling; then move on until all the feelings are addressed and released. This is an amazing process. Canfield suggests writing a "love letter" to get out of the anger and back to the love. Once the negative feelings are released, the bottom line is, "I love you."

Some other tools for dealing with anger include

- Take time out if you are very upset. Going off by yourself can give you a different perspective. Get some physical exercise, or take a shower to cool off.
- Bite your tongue, if you have to, to avoid a cruel tirade.
- Keep it short, focusing on one problem only. Then forgive and forget.
- Separate the behavior from the person. Treat the person with respect and deal with the unacceptable behavior. Use "I-statements." (See Chapter 7.)
- Don't displace anger on an innocent person. If you're mad at your boss, don't take it out on your kids.
- Use active listening skills. (See Chapter 4.)
- Kids can sense your feelings, so be honest. You don't have to

tell them everything; you can say, "Sweetie, I'm angry right now, but I'm not angry at you. It's my problem and I'm working it out." Be truthful but not cruel.
- End on a positive note.
- We must learn to release anger without harming self or others. It is not okay to use emotional or physical violence.
- If your anger is dangerous to you or others, get help.
- Deal with your anger as you'd like others to deal with theirs.

Resentment

Unfinished business from the past has a way of reappearing—nagging at us, demanding attention and resolution. Anger and resentment possess us, punish us, and imprison us in the past. They create tension in our lives and lower our self-esteem. Forgiveness—of ourselves and others—dissolves the tension and releases old pain.

Few people ever mean to be unfair. "If they don't mean it," you might ask, "why do they do it?"

- They may have thought that we deserved it. Many of us heard our parents say, "This hurts me more than it hurts you," as they inflicted punishment. (See Chapter 15.)
- They may have had poor impulse control. Drunk or enraged, they may have unfairly hurt us. They hadn't yet learned responsibility for their own feelings and behaviors.
- Their personal struggles may have spilled over onto the innocent. We may have been in the wrong place at the wrong time and been caught, for example, in the crossfire of a battle between Mom and Dad.
- They may have made mistakes and hurt us even though they had good intentions. They may have bungled or blundered while trying to do their best. A depressed person—with good intentions—may, for example, take his life, creating a great deal of pain for his family.[11]

Resentment has a price. Pain denied and stuffed into the unconscious never loses its power; the wound does not heal. Our challenge is to face the pain squarely, to let go of the past, and to move on with our lives.

> *"The unfairness of the hurt often lies in the experience of the victim, not in the intention of the one who causes it."*
> —Lewis B. Smedes[12]

Forgiveness

Forgiveness has a twofold purpose: to heal you and to heal a damaged relationship. Blaming and resentment trap a part of you in the past—a past that is ancient history and that has no place haunting and interfering with your present life. Letting go lets you heal yourself and your memory.

Our parents were not perfect. Parents, teachers, and other important adults in our lives made mistakes that hurt us. Forgiveness sets us free from the prison of pain we never deserved. We forgive others, but more important, we forgive ourselves.

Feelings are valid: listen to them. After having been "stuffed" for many years, they may seem distorted and exaggerated. Just accept them—allow them to be. Allow *yourself* to feel the pain, the anger, even the hatred that might still be inside. Acknowledging these feelings is the first step toward releasing and resolving them.

One strategy for letting go is to write a letter to the person you resent. Take a moment to get in touch with all the feelings you still have concerning this person. Honestly allow those feelings to flow onto the paper without censoring them, because you really have no intention of mailing this letter. It's for you. If the "old" pain reappears, write another letter. You may need to pound pillows or find a therapist to help you deal with difficult emotions. The next (and absolutely crucial) step is to forgive yourself for having had "negative" feelings—toward others and toward yourself. And know that *you didn't deserve the wounds*.

The process of forgiveness begins with courage and a decision. It calls for willingness to be honest with yourself, to see more clearly and reframe your thinking. Unraveling faulty thinking can help us begin to heal. Many people overgeneralize: this is wrong; that is wrong; therefore, *everything* is wrong! They jump from a few specifics to a global catastrophe: "Everything's totally and completely awful."

To reverse this process, think of someone who is "all bad." Look for the specific behavior that bothers you; then consider all the other attributes that make up this person. What someone *does* is not who he or she *is*. (See Chapter 18.)

Separate who they are from what they did. When examining the pain, be very specific about the harmful incidents. What particular behavior wounded you?

Forgiveness involves a willingness to see with new eyes—to understand and to let go. They did what they did out of their own weakness. You did not deserve it. They could not give you what they did not have. They could not teach you what they did not know.

When you understand that they are not awful people but frail and needy persons who made a painful mistake, you are moving closer to forgiveness. When you can wish them well, you'll know that forgiveness has begun. As you peel off the layers of old hurt, anger, and guilt, underneath you'll discover a beautiful, lovable, more relaxed and capable you.

In examining our old wounds, in releasing the anger and pain, we are insuring that we don't recreate the same wounds in those we love the most. We have all been wounded. Instead of wounding our children, let us heal ourselves.

> *It doesn't matter your age, or your color,*
> *or whether your parents loved*
> *you or not.*
> *(Maybe they wanted to but couldn't.)*
> *Let that go.*
> *It belongs to the past.*
> *You belong to the NOW.*
>
> *It doesn't matter what you have been.*
> *The wrong you may have done.*
> *The mistakes you've made.*
> *The people you've hurt.*
>
> *You are forgiven.*
> *You are accepted.*
> *You are okay.*
> *You are loved—in spite of everything.*
> *So love yourself, and nourish the seed within you.*
>
> *Celebrate you.*
> *Begin NOW.*
> *Start anew.*
> *Give yourself a new birth today. . . .*
> *Today can be a new beginning, a new thing, a new life!*
>
> —Clyde Reid[13]

Gratitude

We all have much to be thankful for. In visiting other countries, I notice many people who appear to be poor yet feel rich. In contrast, many of us appear to be rich, yet feel poor. We don't appreciate how much we do have but instead are anxious about what we don't have.

High-powered television advertising, to which adults and children are subjected, instils in us gnawing dissatisfaction with what we have and desire for what we don't have. Under its spell, we begin to think of our wants as needs. We are talked into *needing* items that we have survived without for many years. No matter how much we have, we are not satisfied; it's never enough. In our culture we lust after material possessions.

Chronic dissatisfaction is brought on by an epidemic of perfectionism. Perfectionists are always wanting something they don't have in order to fulfill their ideal image of being "perfect." This results in a future orientation that precludes deep satisfaction and is hard on true self-esteem.

Gratitude, on the other hand, reduces tension. Focusing on the positive aspects of ourselves, our children, and our parents lowers personal and interpersonal stress. Counting our blessings increases our joy.

We have much to be grateful for. My mother-in-law, Nida, is grateful every morning that she has another day to enjoy, that the birds are singing, that there is food in the refrigerator. Noticing and giving thanks for the "little things" makes her life rich.

A friend of mine pauses before each meal to hold hands around the table with her family and guests and to give thanks—for the food, for each other, for whatever is positive in their lives. Rituals such as this are special times of closeness and appreciation.

With gratitude, we focus on what we do have, not on what we don't. Once we change our focus, we can express gratitude to ourselves and to others. This appreciation and recognition enhances self-esteem.

Emotions can be guides for making necessary and important choices in life. Expressing and accepting responsibility for our feelings is easier for people whose parents accepted their feelings when they were small.

If you have difficulty expressing your feelings, therapy or a support group could be very helpful in dealing with the backlog and learning new skills. It is important to learn how to deal with emotions in a healthy way. Don't keep them to yourself. Find a way to share them; take the risk. If you don't deal with them, they'll deal with you.

Ways to Cope

WHEN YOU ARE FEELING:	AND YOU'RE TEMPTED TO:	CHOOSE A MORE HELPFUL WAY TO COPE:
Nervous	Smoke	Make a list of your strengths
Angry	Lose your temper	Get physical exercise
Lonely	Get in trouble	Talk out your feelings
Wild	Overeat	Take a walk
Disappointed	Turn to drugs or	Do relaxation exercises
Bored	alcohol	Ask for help

Tired
Down on yourself
Hurt
Cheated
Discouraged

Stop eating
Destroy something
Make people angry
Drive too fast
Spend money
Worry so much you
   lose sleep
Get in a fight
Quit trying
Avoid the problem
Skip a meal
Give up

Write a letter to a friend
Do something that makes
   you feel really good
Cook
Listen to music
Dance
Draw or paint
Play sports
Clean a drawer or corner of
   your room
Count to ten
Get involved
Read
Write out how you feel
Plan something to look
   forward to
Rest

Source: This chart is excerpted from Gilda Gussin and Anne Burbaum, *Self-Discovery: Developing Skills* (Boston: Learning for Life Management Sciences for Health, 1984).

Chapter 7

The Power of Words

"A torn jacket is soon mended, but hard words bruise the heart of a child."
—Henry Wadsworth Longfellow[1]

The language parents and teachers choose and the way they use it can determine a child's destiny. Words have the power to lift up or to put down. Words have the power to build or shred self-esteem.

I became aware of this about ten years ago while on a picnic in the mountains with my children. My oldest son, about twelve then, said, "Mom, can I climb that mountain?" I responded, "Okay, Damian," and off he went.

A little later my youngest son (who was about seven) said, "Mom, can I climb that mountain?" I responded, "No, Felix, you're too clumsy." When I heard what I'd said, I tried to pull the words back, but it was too late. I felt terrible!

Back home, Felix began to drop, spill, bump into, and fall over everything. He must have turned my careless statement into his own "self-talk," saying to himself, "That important person who is my mother believes that I'm clumsy; therefore I must be clumsy." It was a self-fulfilling prophecy. He became a walking disaster.

Every time he went to pour milk, it was all over the counter. I was careful not to make an issue out of it; I simply encouraged him to clean it up. After about two weeks he returned to "normal." This experience was my initiation into understanding the power of words.

Since that time, I have learned how to undo clumsy words. I could have undone the harm by saying, "Felix, that was a clumsy thing I said, and I'm sorry," and given him a hug. Then I could have called Damian to take Felix with him up the mountain, or I might have climbed with him myself. Somehow I could have helped him come out winning.

The words that damage self-esteem are spoken without respect for others. The tone of voice is nasty, condescending, and cruel. Often, we "turn up the volume" in hopes of improving listening ability on the other end. More often than not, these strategies are counterproductive. They turn people—kids—into losers.

If you were raised this way, start listening to your own words and to the tone of your voice. Think about who it was that said those things to you. Remember how you felt hearing them. Those old patterns may still be operating in your life.

Fortunately, once you have awareness, you have a choice. You can allow yourself to "go on automatic," to do to your kids what was done to you (even though you hated it), *or* you can become the kind of parent you would like to have had.

Listen to the words coming out of your mouth. What effect do they have on others? What effect do they have on you? Do you really want to do/say those things?

Many times we need to bite our tongues to stop a nasty statement from slipping out. In fact, a bit of scar tissue on the tip of the tongue is like a badge of honor. It means we care enough to stop, to take time to cool off, and then to talk about the problem later when we could tell the kids what we were feeling and what we wanted.

Living in a family requires us to interact with and respond to others. We can do this negatively with criticism or positively with feedback.

Self-Esteem Shredders

Killer statements are most damaging. They should never be used. Examples are

- "Don't be you."
- "You were a mistake."
- "I wish you had been a boy."
- "If I didn't have you, I could have had a career."

Behaviors that convey the same damaging messages are constant ignoring, rejection, battering/abuse, and acting or speaking as if the child were not there when he or she is there. Killer statements are deadly—psychologically and physically. Don't ever use them.

Crooked communication refers to statements that sound positive at first but that have a negative, damaging twist (left-handed compliments). I think of the many greeting cards that look cute and funny on the outside yet are cutting and hurtful on the inside. The statements are often sarcastic, insincere, or patronizing.

- "You're pretty good at math—for a girl."
- "Oh, you *never* make a mistake."
- "You *always* know the answer, don't you?"

Crooked communication is confusing and painful; it erodes self-esteem.

Negative ways of dealing with negative behavior include criticism, put-downs, ridicule, name-calling, blaming, and rejection. "You-statements" are common ("You can't do anything right." "What's wrong with you?" "How could you be so stupid?" "You always get into trouble." "When are you going to grow up?"). They are usually delivered in a nasty tone of voice and are often exaggerated ("You always _____" or "You never _____"). Related to external force (and punishment), you-statements attack the whole person instead of focusing on the problem and desired behavior.[2]

Many of us were raised on you-statements. Take a moment and return to your childhood. Remember times when people spoke to you that way. What did they say to you? How did they say it? What did you feel about yourself? About them? What conclusions did you draw? How did those incidents affect your relationship with the other person(s) involved?

You-statements mostly feel like attacks, and when we feel attacked we want to protect and defend ourselves. We don't want to hear painful words, and we cannot understand how the people who claim to love us can hurt us this way. Instead of being able to respond appropriately, we lock into fear and self-protection, compliance or defiance.

The intent of the parent—to deal with and change behavior—is honorable. The negative methods used to achieve it don't work. You-statements don't teach children what it is that you *do* want. Instead, they teach fear. Children hear you and conclude, "I'm no good." "I can't do anything right." "I'm worthless." "I'm not lovable." "I can't trust you." "You don't care about me." In this process, the self-esteem of both parent and child is damaged, and the relationship between the two may be harmed.

It should be noted that not all you-statements are damaging; for example, "You did a good job!" "You need to finish putting away the dishes," or "You must be proud of yourself."

If you were brought up hearing negative messages, you have probably caught yourself saying things to your children that you swore you never would say. It is hard to change behavior, especially habitual ways of acting and speaking, but it can be done. It begins with awareness, then a commitment, then working at it. The payoff for you and your children will be tremendous.

Many destructive patterns keep repeating themselves simply because we don't know of better ways to deal with problems. It is crucial that we expand our options. In the days when extended families were the rule and not the exception, there were many role models. We could see how Uncle John played with his kids and how Uncle George solved problems with his. Today, with smaller families, we may be unaware of many options available to us because we have never seen them. Let us now discuss some of the positive options that are open to us.

Self-Esteem Builders

Words that build self-esteem are spoken with respect for the other person and with caring about what is going on inside. They are encouraging, and they invite people to become winners. The tone of voice is "clean," not charged with negative emotion. A loving touch—a pat on the back, a hug—often accompanies the words. This is positive feedback.

Positive strokes for being are nourishing and life-giving[3] Feedback can "feed" the spirit, validate others, and make them want to be winners. Read the following statements and be aware of what feelings they evoke in you.

- "You are special and unique."
- "You are important to me."
- "I like you!"
- "I love you."
- "I believe in you."
- "I'm glad you're here."

Nonverbally these are expressed by an attitude of respect and enjoyment, by affection, by taking the children seriously, by spending time with them, and by really listening.

Rewards for doing recognize effort or improvement and show appreciation. Feedback encourages children to do things well.

- "Fantastic!"
- "Atta boy!"
- "It looks like you really worked hard on that."
- "Keep up the good work."
- "Go ahead—try it."
- "Look at the progress you've made."

Many kids and adults have difficulty with compliments. They don't know what to do with them. It's really very simple: someone has given you a gift, so just say thank you. It you trust their sincerity, all you have to do is take a deep breath and let it in.

Positive ways of dealing with negative behavior should be given with respect and caring. It is very important to deal with unacceptable behavior and to invite/encourage children to become winners. We do this by giving them feedback about inappropriate behavior.

The underlying message behind feedback is acceptance, valuing, and inspiring the other to be better. It is a strategy for changing others through guidance, encouragement, and support. Feedback is given as a gift to another out of caring. It is given as a suggestion—something important for the other to consider—rather than an order. It works by motivating the other to be good, by creating a desire in the other person to correct the situation.

As parents we must set reasonable and healthy limits for our children. The most effective way for us to deal with inappropriate behavior is to *separate the behavior from the person*. "They are okay, their behavior is not; we love them, but we do not like what they did."

"I-statements" are an effective way of dealing with undesirable behavior. The model is: "I feel _____ when you _____ because _____, and what I want is _____." ("I feel mad when you leave your shoes on the living-room floor because they make the room look messy, and what I want is for you to put them under your bed.") I-statements are specific, keeping the focus on the behavior, not on the person. They clearly state what it is that you *do* want. With I-statements, children learn cause and effect relationships ("Mom feels _____ because I did _____"), and they learn judgment skills.[4]

Another helpful strategy for dealing with negative behavior is *substitution*. Stop the behavior you don't want; then encourage the behavior you do want. For example, "Don't do _____. Do _____ instead." ("Don't hit your sister; hit a pillow or your punching bag instead.") Another approach is, "Don't do _____. You can figure out a better way to do it." In this way we stop the undesirable behavior and lead the child to more acceptable behavior.

Feedback, well given, feels like a gift. There is no need for defensiveness. The child observes the acceptance, respect, and caring and concludes, "Mom/Dad cares about me enough to tell me this and encourage me to be better. I am important. I am worthwhile." The self-esteem of both parties is enhanced. The language and approach allow the receiver to hear what is being said, and the desired change in behavior is more likely to happen.

	CRITICISM	FEEDBACK
Leadership Style	Autocratic. Respect may be lacking. Little concern about self-esteem.	Democratic. Based on respect for others, concern about the relationship, and self-esteem.
Based on	External pressure or force.	Internal motivation of other.
Underlying Message	You must do things *my way*.	I accept and value you, and encourage you to be better.
Language	You-statements, which may be global: "This is how you are."	I-statements, which are descriptive, specific, and limited.
Strategies	The whole person is blamed, criticized, labeled, put down, rejected. Orders and manipulation. Interactions are charged with emotion.	Information based on my experience of specific behavior is delivered in a respectful, matter-of-fact manner.
Response of Other	Criticism feels like an attack; it arouses fear and self-protection, compliance or defiance.	Feedback, when appropriately given, feels like a gift.
Time Frame	Focuses on the past, even drawing in situations from years ago.	Deals with the present, focuses on the future ("And next time I want _____.").
Outcomes	Disempowerment, damaged relationship, low self-esteem.	Empowerment, enhanced relationship, high self-esteem.

Once you decide to use a better way, you need to break the old habits. When you hear the negative words slip out, stop yourself, and say something like: "I'm sorry! I didn't want to say that. Let me say it over." You can talk it over with your kids or spouse and ask them to remind you when you slip, by saying perhaps, "Replay, Mom," or giving another signal. It is possible to change behaviors. It's a bit easier with support and encouragement from others and from yourself.

Chapter Eight

Parenting Responses That Affect Self-Esteem

"Every time I get in trouble you remind me of everything I've ever done wrong in my life. I'm not too sure what kind of person I am, but you're convincing me I'm bad."
—a junior high school student[1]

We have the power to build self-esteem in children—or to shred it. The words we use fall into four basic types of parenting responses: Nurturing and Structuring Responses, which increase self-esteem, and Marshmallowing and Criticizing Responses, which tear it down.[2] As you read these examples, be aware of how they feel to you.

Situation 1

Twelve-year-old Annie says, "I want to sleep at Janet's tonight. Her parents won't be there, but her sixteen-year-old brother will."

Nurturing Response: "You'd like to have fun with your friend tonight. Invite her to come here for the night."

Structuring Response: "No. Unless her parents are home, you may not spend the night there."

Marshmallowing Response: "Well, I don't like the idea, but I guess just this one time wouldn't hurt."

Criticizing Response: "No! Of course not! What would people think of us? And don't you know what sixteen-year-old boys are after?"

Situation 2

Judith says, "My husband is away on business, and the baby is driving me up the wall."

Nurturing Response: "Ask for help—you deserve it. And the baby needs a mother who is not up the wall. You'll both be better off when you start taking care of yourself."

Structuring Response: "Call someone to get help. Find a church or agency that offers child care. It's important to take care of yourself and your baby."

Marshmallowing Response: "Poor thing. There just isn't any good help available these days. I hope you make it."

Criticizing Response: "If you were a better mother, you wouldn't have that problem!"

Situation 3

Five-year-old Laurie won't clean her room and says, "I hate you, Mom."

Nurturing Response: "Laurie [touching her], I know you don't want to clean your room and that you're mad at me. That's okay. I still love you. Let's both clean our rooms at the same time, and when we finish, we'll go outside and play."

Structuring Response: "We're all part of the family, and we all have chores to do. Cleaning your room is an important way of being part of our team."

Marshmallowing Response: "Maybe when you get bigger you'll be able to do something by yourself, poor thing. I'll do it for you so you'll love me."

Criticizing Response: "You bad girl! Don't you talk to me like that! Get in your room right now, and don't come out until it's perfect!"

Nurturing Responses

Based on respect, love and support, nurturing responses encourage self-responsibility. Parents invite children to get their needs met and offer help in doing so. They believe their kids are winners with the capacity to grow; they give them permission to succeed. I-statements and affectionate touch are used.

Structuring Responses

Also based on respect, structuring responses protect, set limits, and demand performance ("I know you can do it!"). Parents expect and encourage children to be capable and responsible. They encourage them to ask for what they need and want, thereby empowering them.

Nurturing and structuring responses fit together nicely. The underlying message for both is, "You are a valuable resource who can be even better. I encourage and promote your growth." The use of these messages results in cooperation, empowerment, win-win situations, and high self-esteem.

Marshmallowing Responses

Based on judging children to be weak and inadequate, marshmallowing responses disempower while sounding supportive. Blaming other persons, the situation, or fate for the problem, they remove responsibility from the child, inviting dependence and encouraging failure. You-statements are commonly used: "Why don't you quit _____." "You poor thing, there's nothing you can do." "I'll do it for you."

Criticizing Responses

Based on disrespect, they encourage children to fail. Ridicule, put-downs, blaming, fault-finding, comparing, and labeling are common. You-statements are often global: "You always _____." "You never _____." Humor is cruel; touch is hurtful or punishing. Marshmallowing and criticizing responses are damaging to self-esteem. They result in anger and resentment, in passivity, dependence, and powerlessness.

Which response styles did your parents mostly use? Are you glad they treated you that way? Which style do you mostly use? How do you feel about treating your children that way?

Many parents find themselves doing to their kids what they swore they'd never do, then feeling guilty about it. It *is* possible to change your style! And when you let go of the handed-down damaging behavior, your self-esteem will go up, and so will everyone else's. It's not easy to change habits, but *you can do it if you really want to!* You will thank yourself a thousand times over; so will your children—and your grandchildren.

Here are some specific strategies for changing from negative to positive response styles.

• **Change your focus.** Instead of always catching your kids being "bad," catch them being good: what you look for, you find. Once you look for the things they're doing right, you'll be surprised at what neat kids they are. Give them lots of encouragement and support ("Atta boy!") for positive behavior.

We all need "strokes." People prefer to get positive strokes, but they'd rather get negative strokes than nothing at all (being ignored). So focus on and encourage the qualities and behaviors you *do* want.

47

• **Expect the best.** Kids *want* to live up to our expectations—unless these expectations are unrealistic or impossible. Expectations of perfection lead to disappointment and despair. (See Chapter 17.) Marshmallowing and criticizing parents expect the worst—and they get it! Nurturing and structuring parents expect the best—and they get it!

Do you believe that kids are worthless and a bother? If so, you will expect that, look for that, and get that. If, on the other hand, you believe that kids are valuable resources who can become even better, you will expect, look for, and get that. (See Chapter 15.)

• **Give up blaming and fault-finding.** Criticizing parents look for what's wrong, find it, then put down the other person in order to feel one-up and superior. No one likes to be put down, ridiculed, humiliated, or blamed. Criticism leads to resentment and anger—or passivity and dependency. It results in powerlessness and discouragement. Everyone's self-esteem suffers.

Nurturing and structuring parents avoid blaming and fault-finding; they think, instead, in terms of responsibility. Responsibility means "the ability to respond." Everyone is encouraged to assume responsibility for his or her behaviors and their consequences. When a mistake is made, it's not the end of the world—it just needs to be fixed. It's easier for children to assume responsibility when they understand that mistakes are opportunities for learning, not for ridicule.

I recently found a broken canning jar in the kitchen. I could have yelled and blamed someone. Instead I asked who knew about the jar. I needed to be sure there was no broken glass to cut bare feet. In questioning my children I found out that it was broken when my son removed it from the dishwasher, and he hadn't noticed. So together we checked out the machine and removed all the remaining broken glass. We both responded to the situation (assumed responsibility for it) and resolved the problem without anyone's self-esteem being damaged.

We see the results of our parenting responses every day. Let's make a commitment to ourselves and to our children to make our responses nurturing and growth-producing.

Chapter Nine

Parents Are Leaders: Re-Visioning Your Family

"Better one word before than two after."
—Welsh proverb

Probably no one told you that as a parent you are a leader. But you are a leader of great importance! You are a leader with tremendous power. Your challenge is to use this power to create health, happiness, and high self-esteem in your family.

In playing with the idea of leadership, I discovered five basic components. Let's discuss these using the example of leading a horse.

• **Vision/direction/goals.** In leading a horse, I must know where I am going—to the barn. Success is more likely if I consider the needs of the horse. If he's very thirsty, I can almost count on having a power struggle unless I allow him to get a drink as we pass the water tank. Once he gets a drink, we can continue to the barn. When we are sensitive to and respectful of others' needs, we can usually both come out winning.

• **Focus on what I want.** It's important to keep sight of my vision—the barn. I need to focus on what I *do* want, not on what I don't want.

• **Communicate the message.** I must let the horse know what I want and head it toward the barn. Parents are teachers who must clearly communicate to their children what it is they want.

• **Support the desired progress.** As the horse moves in the desired direction, I encourage and support his progress toward the barn.

• **Expect success and get it.** I fully expect that we will get to the barn, and we will.

These components describe *proactive leadership*. Proactive leadership sets out what is wanted in advance and leads the way to it. Most of life's problems can be anticipated and avoided. Proactive leadership (also known as prevention) takes children away from trouble and danger and redirects them to a better, safer activity.

The more common style of leadership is *reactive*. Reactive leadership may seem easier to do (if it has become habitual), yet it creates more difficulty and stress. Many parents don't know what they *do* want for their children, and therefore they don't tell them. The unsuspecting child innocently does something and gets jumped on: "You shouldn't have done that!" The kid is confused and angry because nobody ever told him or her not to do it.

Example: Molly walks past some toys on the bottom stair; Mom reacts by yelling, "Why didn't you take those upstairs?" The answer is that Molly wasn't told and she's not a mind-reader; but of course she doesn't say that. Both parties are angry, and Molly is confused. Parents must clearly communicate what they want in advance. It makes life much easier.

Reactive parents frequently resort to threats, force, criticism, humiliation, ridicule, and punishment, which create negative feelings both in their children and to themselves. Self-esteem plunges. With a little foresight, this is usually preventable.

Examples of Leadership Styles

PROACTIVE LEADERSHIP	REACTIVE LEADERSHIP
• "childproofs" a home as baby begins to toddle	• changes nothing and says no all the time
• removes broken glass from a yard before a foot is cut	• removes broken glass after an accident
• lets a child know that you must leave in fifteen minutes, then perhaps sets a timer for ten minutes	• waits until it's time to leave, then gets angry because the child is not ready
• says, "I hope you'll always let me know where you are and when you'll be back; call me if you're late"	• does not discuss plans and expectations in advance, then yells at a teen when he or she gets home late
• tells children you're going to a restaurant and explains desired behavior	• takes unprepared children to a restaurant, then threatens never to take them to another

The Language of Leadership

PROACTIVE LEADERSHIP	REACTIVE LEADERSHIP
(looks toward the future)	(focuses on the past)
• "That was awful. I know you can do better."	• "Why did you _____?"

- "Next time I want you to _____"
- "Why don't you try _____?"

- "Why didn't you _____?"
- "You shouldn't have _____"

The language of reactive leadership reinforces unwanted behavior by focusing on it. The language of proactive leadership acknowledges and deals with present inappropriate behavior, then leads the child toward improving. It gives another chance while guiding and encouraging progress toward the desired behavior.

Think for a moment about the leadership style of your parents. Was it proactive or reactive? How was it for you? How did it affect your self-esteem? What do you want for your children?

Re-Visioning Your Family

Let's take a closer look at vision/direction/goals—the basis of leadership. What vision have you in mind for your family in five years? In ten years? In fifteen years? In what ways do you want your family to be like the family of your childhood? How do you want it to be different? You have the power not only to create a vision but to live it.

In re-visioning our families, we are led to examine our values. What were the important qualities of the family of your childhood? What was valued? Note which of the following characteristics apply to you.

performance • perfection • work • being "good" • possessions
being who you are • adventure • conformity • trust • authority
avoiding conflict • a clean house • friendships • travel • spontaneity
rules • play • fun • love • choices • acceptance • being obedient
• thinking of yourself • being open and honest • being pretty and clean
being "nice" • being religious • feeling • thinking for yourself
• integrity • family unity • taking care of yourself • not risking
pleasing others • connectedness • isolation • keeping down the pain
respect • responsibility • self-protection • encouragement
discouragement • risking • taking care of others • belonging

Which of these characteristics led to health and happiness for you and your brothers and sisters? Which did not? Which do you now choose for your own family? Keep the vision broad (not "I want my son to be a doctor"), focusing on qualities and values that will enhance your lives. Knowing what you want is the first step in getting it.

Many years ago I had an important insight. I realized that if I trusted outside voices more than my inner voice (see Chapter 19) when values clashed, I would be teaching my children values that I didn't believe in and create confusion and conflict. Specifically, I believe that force and violence are wrong, yet my children were learning from many sources that violence was an accepted way to get what they wanted. I realized that it was important to reexamine and clarify all my values, to pass on those that I truly believed in and discard those that were not really meaningful to me.

Once you have your own vision of a Winning Family, take a small step every day in that direction. Believe in your vision; then communicate it. This can be done in many ways. For example, when my daughter Kristen was small, I said to her, "One day you'll be a beautiful, strong woman." To my sons I said, "Someday you'll grow up to be wonderful, gentle men." Without realizing it at the time, I was planting seeds of my vision in my children. Now, as adults, each is sensitive and each is strong.

After communicating, you'll need to guide, encourage and support them. Then celebrate and be thankful for the little steps of progress toward the vision.

> *A leader is best*
> *When people barely know that he exists,*
> *Not so good when people obey and acclaim him,*
> *Worst when they despise him.*
> *"Fail to honor people,*
> *They fail to honor you."*
> *But of a good leader, who talks little,*
> *When his work is done, his aim fulfilled,*
> *They will all say, "We did this ourselves."*
>
> —Lao Tsu

Chapter Ten

Parenting Leadership Styles

*"To revere power above everything else
is to be willing to sacrifice everything else to power."*
—Marilyn French[1]

The leadership style you employ affects the type of child you raise and the self-esteem of your family. Think for a moment about the leadership style of your parents. Was there a rigid structure with very little freedom or flexibility *(autocratic—parents keeping and overusing power)*? Were there too few rules and limits and too much freedom and flexibility *(permissive—parents abdicating power)*? Or was there a balance of firmness, freedom, and caring *(democratic—shared power)*?

AUTOCRATIC	DEMOCRATIC	PERMISSIVE
MOST	CONTROL/STRUCTURE/GUIDANCE	LEAST

These styles reflect different uses of power and control—from overpowering at the left to abdicating at the right.

Love is the other dimension of parenting. (see Chapter 2.) Love enhances each leadership style, making it healthier for the family. Add love to the autocratic style, and it becomes authoritarian *and* caring, more positive and less damaging. The permissive style without love and support is neglect. Love is the baseline for mental health and successful family life.

After you've identified your parents' leadership style, reflect on how it affected you. Did you like it? Was it good for you? What kind of a relationship do you now have with your parents? Is that what you want to have with your children when they grow up?

Often, children who dislike their parents' style vow that they will bring up their own children differently. Many swing from one extreme to the other, creating a new family perhaps with as many problems, only different ones. This swing is commonly from the autocratic to the permissive style.

Autocratic Leadership Style

Characteristics of Parents

Autocratic or "drill sergeant" parents impose their will through a rigid structure of rules, allowing little flexibility or freedom. They tend to

- overuse or abuse power
- always strive to be one-up
- take total control and responsibility for all decisions and rules
- take charge of other people's lives
- think that their way is the only right way
- withhold information
- be out of touch with their feelings (or shut them down)
- ignore or put down the opinions and feelings of others; e.g., "You're too sensitive."
- use pressure and punishment to force compliance
- hurt others

Autocratic parents demand "respect" (which sometimes translates as "fear"). They commonly believe that children should be seen and not heard.

Feelings of Parents

Autocratic parents generally feel

- superior (one-up)
- distrust (or lack of trust)
- burdened with all the responsibility they have chosen to assume
- lonely
- low self-esteem

Feelings of Children

In this type of family configuration, children tend to feel

- out of control
- powerless and helpless

- submissive and dependent or hostile and angry
- unimportant
- self-rejecting
- lonely, with low self-esteem

These children feel afraid and guilty, yet they don't know what to do with their feelings since they are ignored or denied by their parents.

Characteristics of Children

Placed in a one-down, inferior position to their parents (even when grown), these children work hard at second-guessing, trying to figure out how to *please* their parents and avoid getting punished. They

- want to be told what to do
- lack a sense of personal control and responsibility over their lives
- may distrust their feelings because they've been told those feelings are "wrong"
- lack creativity
- are compliant and withdrawing (accepting powerlessness) or defiant and rebellious (fighting for power)
- may withdraw by moving or running away

One young mother reported that she had rebelled against her autocratic parents by getting pregnant and keeping her baby. Feeling powerless in every other aspect of her life, she asserted control over her own body. Another woman dealt with her autocratic parents by moving to Japan. The autocratic leadership style may work for a period of time, but tends to break down when children become teenagers.

Permissive Leadership Style

Characteristics of Parents

In the very permissive family, there is *too much* freedom. Parents abdicate power, and there are often no rules, limits, or structure. If rules do exist, they are always changing, which results in chaos. Permissive parents may

- believe they have no rights
- condone everything their children do
- not be interested in their children or what they do

- be physically or emotionally absent and uninvolved
- neglect their children

Feelings of Parents

These parents tend to feel

- discouraged
- confused
- out of control over their lives
- angry
- overwhelmed
- low self-esteem

Feelings of Children

Children in these families often feel

- confused and discouraged
- powerless and helpless
- not taken care of
- angry
- dependent
- out of control
- insecure
- unloved
- low self-esteem

Surrounded by confusion and inconsistency, these children don't feel they can trust their parents.

Characteristics of Children

In permissive families, children

- have trouble with limits (while at the same time craving them)
- lack self-discipline and responsibility (or may have had to assume too much responsibility too soon)
- may take on the unhealthy role reversal of taking care of their parents because their parents won't take care of them
- are often on their own before they are ready
- think they have the right to do exactly as they wish (with little awareness of social responsibility)
- may later be attracted to cults

It is possible that these children will become violent toward their parents.

Democratic Leadership Styles

Characteristics of Parents

Democratic families are based on respect (defined as "admiration for a person or quality"). *Everyone's* needs are considered important. Parents offer choices and treat children as capable, worthwhile human beings who are able to think for themselves and make good decisions. There is a balance of power between husband and wife; neither is solely "the boss." Democratic parents

- give their children many choices and let them learn from the consequences
- provide structure while allowing flexibility and freedom
- invite and encourage children to participate in planning and decision making, yet enforce the rules
- teach responsibility by giving it
- encourage children to learn from mistakes and fix them

Democratic parents function as counselors and coaches. This style—when based on love—is the framework for a winning family.

Feelings of Parents

Democratic parents start from an attitude of cooperation with their children. They

- feel respectful and respected, loving and loved
- trust their children and themselves
- have high self-esteem

Feelings of Children

In democratic families, children know they are responsible for themselves and their behavior. They feel

- trusted and respected
- worthwhile and useful
- self-confident
- self-respecting

They have a high level of self-esteem

Characteristics of Children

Having a team sense, these children are eager to cooperate. They

- respect rules
- are self-disciplined and responsible
- understand cause-effect relationships
- are capable and self-determining

Through making choices and decisions, children of democratic families learn to direct their own lives. They have a friendly relationship with their parents that will someday become a relationship between equals.

A husband and wife attending my workshop came to the realization that *he* was authoritarian and *she* was permissive. The more he swung one way, the more she swung the other. This was confusing to their children and difficult for the whole family. With this insight into their conflict, this couple had an opportunity to make new choices.

A teenage girl talked about life in her autocratic family: "Often it gets to the point where home seems like a concentration camp, and it becomes a challenge to 'escape.' Tension builds to a disastrous point, with too much emphasis put on chores. People start fighting and hurting each other." She continued in a letter to her parents, "Don't make chores the most critical and important factor in the household. Don't judge kids on their ability or concern about chores. Coach and help them without exerting power and forcing them to buckle under your iron will. Try to understand each child's needs, other obligations, physical capabilities, attention span, and allow reasonable leeway for these considerations.

"If anger should arise, restrain yourself, and under no circumstances call your children names as you have done in the past. Children and teenagers are highly susceptible to labels: if you call him incompetent, he *thinks* he is, and therefore *becomes* incompetent. If you call him stupid, lazy, slow, useless, clumsy, or irresponsible, he is. He can be devastated by one careless word thrown in anger. Avoid that anger, and keep your children feeling worthy and confident, making each chore simply a duty rather than a futile struggle."

It seems that the autocratic family would be appropriate and fitting under an autocratic government. The permissive family suits a nation where anarchy prevails. In our democratic society, where people must be able to make decisions, think for themselves, and vote for their leaders, the democratic family builds the skills, responsibility, and sense of teamwork that is needed. As parents, we are not actually building "cathedrals"—rather, we are supplying our children with the best quality materials available so they can design and build them themselves.

The autocratic family was the only style that I knew, and therefore it was the style that I "naturally" employed with my young family. As they grew and became able to think, communicate, and be more responsible, I found that I could "loosen up." I gradually let go of my need to be in control, and they were ready and willing to assume more control and responsibility for themselves. As I trusted them more, they became more trustworthy; as they became more trustworthy, I trusted them more. Shifting from external control to motivation from within, I gradually evolved into a democratic leadership style. We were becoming a team. In retrospect, I can see that what I did is in harmony with the second basic dimension of a healthy family. (See Chapter 2.) When children are little, we have total responsibility for their care and protection. As they grow and develop, we can gradually turn over or share the power and responsibility with them.

Power comes from the Latin word *poder,* meaning "to be able." Everyone needs to be able, to be capable, to have a sense of personal power. Democratic parents share power with their children, creating a relationship based on mutual empowerment—instead of mutual victimization. At the heart of personal power is the knowledge that you are in charge of your life—that you have the ultimate responsibility for how you live it. In accepting more and more responsibility for your own self and your behavior, you gain personal power. When we teach kids that they can choose who they want to be and do what they want to do with their lives, we are empowering them. This empowerment is necessary for mental health, for making dreams come true, for self-esteem.

Chapter Eleven

Discipline Without Damage

"Why do I so frequently need to be protected from those who love me?"
—Ashleigh Brilliant[1]

"Spare the rod and spoil the child"—we all heard it when we were young. Most people understood it to mean that if you didn't want a spoiled child, obnoxious and nasty, it was necessary to use physical punishment periodically.

Some biblical scholars recently did research on the origin of this saying. They discovered that shepherds in biblical times had two tools—a staff and a rod. Contrary to modern belief, the rod was not used for hitting; it was used to guide the sheep in the desired direction.

Looking at the statement with new eyes, it is obvious that we need to guide and direct children as we raise them. If we do not, they will certainly be "spoiled." It is tragic that the original meaning has been misinterpreted and is often used to justify domestic violence. In an attempt to not spoil children, parents have damaged them.

The word *discipline* is also frequently misinterpreted. When I ask parents what comes to mind when they hear that word, they respond with "punishment," "force," and "hitting." Yet the word *discipline* has the same root as the word *disciple,* meaning *pupil* or *learner.* The purpose of discipline is to teach in such a way that children can learn and to help them develop their *inner* guidance system so they can function responsibly by themselves. They need to learn self-discipline with little things so they have the strength to deal with larger issues later on.

The short-term goal of discipline is to guide behavior on a daily basis and to protect them from hurting themselves and others. In the long run, discipline should help children take over the responsibility for their own behavior. They need to learn to rely on themselves. This process takes time.

Natural and Logical Consequences

In the past, children grew up in a world in which natural consequences were a daily experience. If you conscientiously tended your garden, there would be a bountiful harvest. If you neglected to milk the cow, she would dry up. The connections were direct and clear.

Individuals in families, neighborhoods, and communities functioned as parts of interdependent systems, and were accountable to each other. Extended families provided diverse role models, and there was a sense of connection even between unrelated adults and children.

Today, children have fewer adults involved in their lives. Interaction time with parents is minimal; children spend countless hours a week in front of the TV. Most television programs do not teach natural consequences—what happens *after* the program ends. Children miss learning about the cause-effect, action-reaction cycles of life. Since we are more removed from the lessons of *natural* consequences, we must rely on *logical* consequences in teaching these skills.

Logical consequences are structured situations based on mutual rights and mutual respect that permit children to learn from the reality of the social order. For example, one day while I was doing errands with my young children, they started fighting in the back seat of the car. I was distracted and irritated and could easily have yelled at them, "You're going to lose your allowance," "You're grounded," or some other threat of punishment. Instead, I pulled the car off the road. Very soon they stopped and asked, "What happened, Mom?" I softly explained that I couldn't drive with so much noise because it distracted me; I would have to wait until they quieted down. It worked like a charm.[2]

It's important to have fair rules and to state them clearly so everyone understands. It's also important that children see the connection between cause and effect—rowdiness, for example, causes Mom to pull the car off the road.

When they know what is expected and don't comply with the rules, they learn from the consequences of their behavior. When they know what is expected and comply with the rules, there can be a sense of accomplishment, importance, and increased self-esteem.

Rescue Behavior

It is easy to interrupt the natural process of learning from consequences. When we rescue others, they miss out on important lessons. The undesirable behavior is therefore likely to be repeated.

Rescue Behavior

	CASE 1	CASE 2
Action	Child turns off alarm.	Child spends money without anticipating future needs.
Result	Oversleeps, misses school bus.	Wants money for activity; has no money left.
Logical Consequence	Child must walk, bike, or take city bus; is late for school.	Child misses activity or has to earn extra money.
Rescuing Action	Parent drives child to school.	Parent gives child money.

The choice not to rescue takes a strong commitment to helping children learn about life from their own behavior and from the social system. It must be appropriate both to the age and maturity level of the child and to the situation. It must also be done in an atmosphere of dignity and respect, love and firmness.

There are times when every parent chooses to practice rescue behavior. Sometimes situations occur that are damaging or difficult for a child to handle. A child being bullied or abused may not have the internal resources to deal with it. There are times when we need to rescue our children.

There may be times when grownups need to be rescued, too. Sometimes life deals us a hard blow; it's wonderful to know there are people we can call on when we're down and out. People get stronger by asking for help and support once in a while—until they get the strength to move on. The problem occurs when rescuing becomes a way of life, when someone always looks to others to take charge and solve problems. This behavior pattern disempowers, weakens and creates low self-esteem and dependency.

Rewards and punishment

"The fundamental issue is not punishment at all, but the development of morality—that is, the creation of conditions that not only allow but strongly induce a child to wish to be a moral, [self-] disciplined person."
—Bruno Bettelheim[3]

Most of us at one time or another have experienced the reward and punishment system. It is based on external control, relying heavily on fear, anger, disappointment, and guilt. Some of its major disadvantages are

- Parents are assumed to be responsible for their children's behavior. They consider the children's performance or misbehavior to be a reflection on them. The parent feels guilty for a child's mistakes and asks, "Where did I go wrong?"
- Parents make all the rules and decisions and expect compliance, which almost inevitably leads to resistance.
- Children are prevented from making their own judgments and decisions and therefore from defining their own standards of behavior.
- Parents use negative strategies to enforce their will: yelling, ridicule, criticism, blame, put-downs, labeling—all of which damage self-esteem.
- If a behavior is controlled by an authority figure, it usually lasts only while the authority figure is present.

When looking at rewards and punishment, it is important once again to remember that children observe then conclude. More often than not, the "lessons" children learn from punishment are not at all what the parents had hoped to teach. A thirty-four-year-old woman told me that she vividly remembers the time her parents sent her down to the bottom basement stair to finish her dinner after she complained that she couldn't chew the meat left on her plate because it was too gristly. When I asked her what she learned from that, she said, "I learned that my parents didn't believe me, even if I was telling the truth. I learned that *I* was less important than their 'clean your plate' rules, and I hated them for humiliating me."

The intention of the parent is to stop unacceptable behavior. The intention of punishment is to hurt the child—physically, mentally, or emotionally—in order to "teach him a lesson." When children are deliberately hurt by parents whom they trust, love, and depend upon, they receive a powerful negative message. Observing and feeling their mistreatment, they may conclude that

- They are not okay. They are bad.
- They deserve to be punished.
- They cannot trust the parent.
- They don't deserve love; they deserve hate.
- That parent hates them.
- It's okay to hurt people.
- The world is not a safe place.
- Their parents are bad, cruel.

Think back to a time when you were punished as a child. What were your feelings toward your parent(s)? What did you learn? How did you feel about yourself?

When parents vow "to teach her a lesson," a kid probably learns fear, distrust, hatred. When parents use force and violence, kids either learn that violence is acceptable to get people to do what you want or they learn to be victims.

Rewards may not seem on the surface to be as potentially damaging as punishment, but they often produce similar results. Children begin to feel manipulated; they learn that they have to "perform" to win their parents' attention and approval. They learn to become people pleasers. After a time, they come to resent the rewards as much as the punishments.

Many parents are in the habit of using the reward and punishment system. They often repeat what *their* parents did, even though they hated it. They may not be aware of the many options available to them.

- Suggestions ("It might be a good idea ____.)
- Asking for a favor or a change in behavior
- Saying no ("No, you may not do that.")
- Communicating clearly what you want and how important it is to you

• Playfulness (such as turning a toddler's spoon into an airplane full of food, or overdramatizing great disgust and nausea on finding dirty underwear in the bathroom). When I would take a walk with my children and noticed their untied shoelaces, rather than make an issue of it, I would playfully try to step on the laces until they got the message.

There are many ways to get what we want. The methods above focus on *internally motivating the other*. They succeed in getting things done with everyone's self-esteem intact.

With rewards, as with punishment, children learn to focus on trying to please those who have power over them, whether they want to or not: "I will do _____ so you will think I'm okay." When parents use their power over kids, the kids feel manipulated. With the reward approach, for example, a kid might get a star for getting dressed and a scolding for being slow. A better approach is to peek in on their progress, saying "Hooray, you got your shoes on. Good for you, you're almost ready." Celebrate their progress, their growth. This reflects their small achievements back to them and helps them to intrinsically feel good about themselves. Tomorrow they may tell themselves (self-talk) the same thing: "Good for me, I'm almost ready."

With the reward system, tomorrow the child may again want a star or some other bribe to externally motivate him to get dressed. This outside focus leads to the development of external locus of control people (see Chapter 19), who lack self-confidence and always look to others to tell them what to do.

Rewards, in moderation, are okay. Don't stop rewarding your kids. The ultimate goal, though, is for the child to want to get dressed, practice piano, keep his room clean for himself, without involving time or energy on the parent's part. This attitude is more likely to result from the encouragement/support method.

Physical punishment doesn't change someone's mind. It may change behavior for a while, but it doesn't change their opinion or thinking about what they're doing. Fear is a poor motivator.

When people are blamed and punished, they feel as if they have been attacked or violated. They may react by

• being defensive
• making excuses
• trying to protect themselves
• wanting to withdraw
• being afraid
• giving in (complying)

- becoming defiant
- seeking perfection ("If I were perfect, I might be okay.")
- lying, cheating, or covering up

Once parents decide that they want children to be self-disciplined, they must discipline themselves to change old, punishing patterns of behavior and to model new behaviors. Once parents decide that they do not need to control—that they can trust children to learn from the consequences of their behavior they can give up rewards, punishments, and the associated feelings of distrust and resentment. They can move from an autocratic to a more democratic leadership style. With the natural/logical consequences approach,

- children are responsible for their own behavior.
- they are allowed to make their own decisions and to learn from their successes and their mistakes.
- children learn from the reality of the natural and social order rather than from forced compliance to the wishes of authority figures.

This system of discipline focuses on the whole child, not only on behavior. The goal is to teach *self*-discipline, *self*-direction, and *self*-responsibility. Since parents won't always be around to tell children what to do, they must instil *inner* discipline and help the children develop the ability to think, to judge, and to make decisions on their own. They must also model the behavior they want to see in their children: example is the best teacher.

"It is easier to control than to teach," writes Dr. Stephen Glenn, an author and national consultant. "Teaching requires time, planning and patience, but it lasts longer, gives clearer direction, and builds a foundation for a system of value. Dogs need to be controlled. Children need to be taught."[4]

Parents must realize that every kid is frisky and mischievous at times. It is how they express their individuality and aliveness. If they want to do something and it doesn't hurt them, let them do it. Give in on the little things. All normal kids act out once in a while; they are testing their environment. It's important to allow them self-expression while also setting limits.

When I had two little ones, I used a name—"Boobledink"—to express mild displeasure. If, for example, someone would poke a finger in the icing of a birthday cake, I'd say, "You Boobledink," with partly serious displeasure. Even now I sometimes call my grown children that, and we laugh about it.

It's important to be aware of the degree of seriousness of the mischief. If it's serious, it should be dealt with, but there may be wisdom in letting little things slide. We need to choose our battles carefully.

It's also important to look for the cause of undesirable behavior and deal with that. Misbehavior is a signal that something isn't right; your child, for example, may need attention, or be discouraged, or feel powerless. Get to the underlying feelings. (See Chapter 6.) Help them to talk it out so they don't have to act it out.

The democratic family is a family where no one has to lose. It is a winning team in which parents are coaches who are positive, encouraging, and correcting when necessary. Kids need attention, feedback, and the awareness that they are fulfilling your expectations. Parents who are coaches get positive results.

Coaches expect the best in their players and communicate that to their team. They believe in them and inspire them to greatness. The team members don't want to disappoint the coach, so they do their best.

Coaches are teachers who explain how to do things better. One dad, for example, observed his daughter using a hammer. Seeing her ineffectiveness, he stopped her, took the hammer, and showed her the correct way to use it. Giving it back to her, he asked her to try it that way. As she hammered more effectively, Dad encouraged her and celebrated her success.

Look for opportunities to share your knowledge and your skills. You know so much, and your children have so much to learn. Teaching them sets up positive contact between you.

Finally, coaches spend time correcting undesirable and unacceptable behavior. They do that without discouraging or demoralizing the player. In *The One-Minute Manager,* Kenneth Blanchard and Spencer Johnson[5] outline this simple plan

1. Let them know you want them to learn and grow and that you will correct them at times. Correcting them does not mean you don't like them or that you're rejecting them but that there's a better way. (See Chapter 18.)
2. It is best to correct behavior while it's happening or as soon as you are aware of it. Deal with them in private.
3. Tell them that what they did was not acceptable. Describe the behavior, being specific, firm, and kind.
4. Tell them what you think and feel about that behavior, being clear but not angry.
5. Pause and let it soak in.
6. Touch them, smile, or say kind words to show you have not

rejected them, that you are on their side. Tell them that you value them but that the specific behavior is unacceptable.
7. Forgive and forget it. It's over.

We must deal with unacceptable behavior—in our kids, spouses, and friends and in ourselves. How we do this makes a difference.

> *If I keep from commanding people, they behave themselves.*
> *If I keep from preaching at people, they improve themselves.*
> *If I keep from imposing on people, they become themselves.*
>
> —Lao Tsu

Chapter Twelve

Guidance

"Lead me from the unreal to the real! Lead me from darkness to light!"
—Upanisbads

Every culture has teachings that are transmitted from parent to child. On a trip to Nepal, I visited a village at the edge of a jungle inhabited by rhinos, tigers, and wild boars. In the river there were crocodiles! Children growing up in that environment learn very early about the dangers surrounding them.

Everyone in the village knows that the rhinos leave their feeding ground after dark to go elsewhere to sleep. The young must be taught—as I was taught—to stay off the path when the rhinos might be there. They must learn how to avoid dangerous animals and, if necessary, how to deal with them. Nepalese children know what to do if they meet a rhino—they climb a tree fast!

Few American parents have to teach their kids how to deal with rhinos. Children need their guidance in many other ways. As parents we need to forewarn our children and protect them from the numerous hazards built in to our environment. There are poisons under the kitchen sink and in the medicine cabinet, chemical pollutants seeping into the water we drink, and nuclear pollutants escaping into the air we breathe. Never before has a generation of children wondered whether they would live to become adults!

The social world is also very frightening. Parents are concerned about the dangers that seem to lurk just beyond the playground corner. And kids are scared, too. Instead of indulging ourselves in worry, we need to turn our concern into positive action.

Children look to parents for guidance. They want it, and they need it. In the past, parents were the primary teachers of values, appropriate behavior, and lifeskills. Children used to spend most of their waking hours interacting with parents, grandparents, and other members of their extended family. Now they spend most of their waking hours watching television.

A study done in Boston revealed that by the time a child reaches age eighteen, he or she has viewed 350,000 commercials. The average

73

American watches television six hours and twenty minutes per day. During those many hours, they sit back and wait for things to happen; they are passive and uninvolved. They take in whatever happens to be showing, whether they like it or not, whether it's true or not, whether it's healthy or not. At the time of life when their minds are most impressionable and receptive, they are being parented by television.

As a project for an anthropology class, I joined my children (then eight through twelve years old) for Saturday morning cartoons. Within three hours, we counted forty-two commercials, mostly aimed at influencing children's food choices and parents' buying habits. Together we rated the quality and agreed that only two of the programs were amusing; the rest were mediocre to poor, often using slapstick or violence as humor. By about 11:00 A.M., I was beginning to feel a bit nauseous (and a little "crazy"), so I turned it off. My kids protested, saying, "Mom, maybe the next one will be better."

A report by the University of Pennsylvania's School of Communication recently stated that the "family hour" on TV (which has the most children viewers) is really the "violence hour." The programs of the three major networks include 168 acts of violence per week. This is the highest rate of violence in the nineteen years since the study was first conducted in 1967.[1] More people see the worst TV program than would see a Broadway show playing to a full house for twenty years.

Advertisers, in their competition for the consumer dollar, are becoming more and more skillful at manipulating the viewing public. They have confused us and undermined our self-esteem, blurring the distinction between real and artificially manufactured "needs." Traveling to other countries points up the absurdity of our consumer mentality. We do not *need* designer clothes and VCRs; kids do not *need* Cabbage Patch dolls. Our real needs are rather simple: food and shelter, safety, belonging, love, respect, self-esteem. All other "needs" are really only wants/desires/wishes—or things we're being talked into thinking we want. (See Chapter 19.)

The hours spent viewing TV are hours not available for actively participating in the real world, or playing, or being involved with friends and family. Watching television is an individual activity that tends to discourage interaction with others; as viewing time increases, family communication time decreases. As family communication decreases, people grow more distant from each other and may even forget how to carry on a good conversation.

Young children need to learn about life, about how this world works, about how to think, feel, and behave. Impressionable and trusting, they watch television to learn appropriate behavior, skills, and values. Information and misinformation alike become part of their reality, their belief system. They are innocent; they are vulnerable.

The unconscious cannot distinguish between fact and nonfact, between fantasy and reality. It accepts everything as truth, even that which is not true. (See Chapter 16.) In good faith, children take in and believe what they are "taught." They may be more likely to internalize TV values than to believe their own experience—or what their parents teach them. This TV version of reality can and does lead to confusion, pain, and addiction. For children raised on a heavy TV diet, television replaces direct firsthand experiencing and becomes their reality.

When children look to television to learn about life, what do they learn? They learn to become consumers—never to be satisfied with what they have, always to "need" more things; then they become frustrated and angry if they cannot afford them. They learn to crave sugar. They learn to seek immediate gratification of their desires, to use violence to solve problems—or they learn to be passive and uninvolved with life. They also learn that

- Happiness comes from material possessions and external conditions.
- Drugs will cure everything.
- Violence is exciting and acceptable behavior.
- Our homes are infested with dirt and invisible enemies that the housewife must continually work to eliminate.
- Skinny is beautiful, but women's bodies are never okay as they are.

These ideas are all setups for low self-esteem. They are accepted in good faith by children hungry to understand life and how they should be in their world. Their minds are filled with misinformation that they consider to be true.

A task force of the American Academy of Pediatrics concluded after a sixteen-month study that

- "Repeated exposure to TV violence can make children both violent and accepting of real-life violence.
- "TV-watching promotes obesity. . . .
- "TV encourages the use of drugs, alcohol and tobacco by glamorizing them.
- "TV's unrealistic sexual relationships may contribute to the risk of teen pregnancy."[2]

TV producers and programmers have no commitment to the guidance of our children. Their only commitment is to their advertisers—to get viewers to buy products. They accept no responsibility for the immense impact of TV on our children.

I remember life before television. As kids we had lots of time to play—times that were perhaps the happiest of my childhood. We would roller-skate and bike and go on snakehunts. We learned to entertain ourselves. With television, all this changed.

People who grow up without television gain firsthand, hands-on experience of the world. They spend more time actively interacting with people and participating in life. They have a more solid foundation.

We learn from everything; so do children. Do you trust TV to teach your children? Find out what your children watch on television. Get involved—choose what you watch together. There are many fine programs on science, art, culture, entertainment, music, and sports. Help your kids select the best, and limit viewing time. Properly regulated TV can enhance your family's life—as can many other activities.

I recently heard a story about someone who visited a home while the children were watching a mystery on TV. Suddenly there were cries of "Don't do it!" "Don't hurt him!" Questioning the mother, the visitor found out that she would turn off programs at the onset of violence.

Children need the benefit of our experience, our wisdom, and our protection so they won't be damaged or destroyed. They need our proactive leadership to help them avoid or deal with the hazards of daily living. When we actively guide them, we steer them away from many potential problems and the resulting stress and trauma.

Children also need guidance to understand themselves and the world they live in, to help them handle their physical, social, and sexual development. It takes courage for parents to talk about some of these things. But if kids can't talk with their own parents, who *will* they talk to? What will they learn? Will it be too late?

Through guidance, we can save our children from preventable pain and nudge them to become healthy, responsible people with high self-esteem.

"If not you, who? If not now, when?"
—Hillel

Chapter Thirteen

Problem Solving

"To the question of your life, you are the only answer.
To the problems of your life, you are the only solution."
—Jo Coudert[1]

As a child I did not know how to solve problems. When I had misunderstandings with my friends, I would not play with them again—or at least, not until we forgot about it. At home when my brother teased me, I ran to my mother, wanting her to protect and rescue me—and punish him. I didn't learn to face problems and get through them. I was unprepared for the challenges of the world, and I was afraid of them.

As a mother, I didn't want my kids to pull me into the middle of every argument they had. I wanted them to be able to solve their own disagreements by themselves. A mother of many adopted children once told me her secret formula: whenever two children had a problem, she had them sit on a certain stair—"the stair of love and peace"—until they worked it through; then they could go play. Those children learned to resolve problems by themselves.

I tried this on my own children. Although they hated it at first, they soon learned that they were responsible for solving their own problems. In effect, I stepped aside and allowed them to develop important skills. In solving their little problems, they gained the skills, experience, and confidence to solve the tougher problems of life.

Problems and conflicts are natural events in life. Everyone has them. We don't choose hassles; we do choose how to deal with them. Some strategies escalate and cause distance, distress, and low self-esteem. Other strategies deescalate and bring about resolution, closeness, and joy. Without skills and confidence, every problem is a crisis. With skills and confidence, a problem is an event to deal with and get beyond.

We're not responsible for solving other people's problems. We can listen as they talk them through. This in itself may alleviate the problem—letting them know someone cares enough to listen and helping them to hear themselves, to get a different perspective. Then, instead of telling them what they should do, we can ask what they think will help resolve the issue. Our en*courage*ment may give them the courage to work it through on their own.

Children need to learn to take care of their own problems and to overcome them. They need to learn to deal with disappointments, losses, and pain so that they know they can survive them. It can be difficult for us as parents to watch them struggle; we want to take away the pain. Yet children who have been overprotected will be incapacitated and overwhelmed by the first real problem they have to handle on their own. Kids who don't know how to deal with failure, disappointment, or loss are kids at risk.

We need to encourage and support children through their struggles—and believe in them. ("I've seen you solve some tough problems; I know you can get through this one, too.") We need to allow them to experience their own mistakes and failures and to help them discover the joy of overcoming. It is not problems or stress that overwhelm kids but self-doubt and lack of experience and skills.

We need to share our own struggles with our children. If we pretend to have it together all the time, they may conclude that something's wrong with them for having problems. When we share our mistakes, our losses, our failures, and how we deal with them, they understand that we, too, experience disappointments—that we, too, are human. And they learn new ideas for coping.

Adults and children alike have basic human needs, including safety, love, belonging, and esteem. If we ignore these needs, problems result. When we attend to these needs, we avoid potential problems. Toddlers, for example, have a need to explore their environment. In childproofing my apartment, I left a few pretty but durable objects out. My first child, Damian, could touch those things—but with only one finger. We both got our needs met. Had I thwarted his need to explore and touch, I would have created problems.

In dealing with family problems, it's important to listen to each other, to understand the situation clearly, and to have the willingness and courage to make changes. When all parties assume responsibility for the problem *and* the resolution, there's hope for a positive outcome.

One adolescent exhibited problem behavior as a result of the stresses of her family situation. She wrote

My "family" became a constant clash of rage caused and aggravated by lying, mistrust, and hurtful accusations. I feel that I was driven out by hatred based on something I don't understand. As my family was self-destructive, it became clear that steps had to be taken to alleviate or avoid further stress. We created commotions, such as fussing, threatening, and running away (behaviors we had never before even considered), desperate for a listening ear. We pleaded for either a solution or an escape and ended up escaping from the problems which were beyond our control.

Her "misbehavior" was merely a symptom of the real problem that her parents refused to discuss or get help for. Running away from home was the best solution to a family problem beyond her control.

It is important to understand that there are always reasons— thoughts and feelings—underneath problems and misbehavior. Problems and misbehavior are but signals that indicate that something is wrong. In order to resolve them effectively, we must deal with the underlying cause and not just react to the symptoms.

Barriers to Problem Solving

One reason that people are afraid of problems is that they don't know how to solve them. They may be using one of these strategies

- **Denial.** This ostrich approach changes nothing; it merely puts things aside for a while. ("No, no! Nothing's wrong.")
- **Drugging.** This strategy alters the inner reality—the *perception* of the problem. With alcohol and other drugs, people can pretend that they've solved the problem because they can no longer feel it. Unfortunately, they are creating a more serious problem.
- **Distraction.** This strategy of avoidance can be a short- or long-term escape from the problem. ("Let's watch TV.")
- **Gunnysacking.** Storing up the problems, anger, and pain solves nothing. When it builds up, a harmful explosion may result.
- **Blaming.** When we point our finger at others and resort to fault-finding, we deny our own responsibility and our ability to change things. The persons who are blamed feel attacked and want to either defend themselves or retaliate.
- **Rejection.** Cutting people off may *seem* to solve a problem, but an important relationship can be damaged or lost. ("I never want to see you again.")

- **Fighting/Withdrawing.** One is aggressive; the other is passive. In our culture boys are often taught to slug it out, while girls learn to seek help or wait to be rescued. ("Put up your dukes!" or "Mommy! Help me!")
- **Personal attacks.** Name-calling and you-statements hurt the other, escalate the conflict, and often harm the relationship. ("You are totally worthless.")
- **Rationalizing.** This strategy intellectualizes the pain to avoid feeling it. ("We're better off than the neighbors.")
- **Defeatism.** If you believe there is nothing you can do to solve the problem, you will not be able to do anything. ("It's hopeless.")

These are strategies for living with—not dealing with—problems. They are very common, and they get us stuck. They don't work because they avoid the problem. Avoidance is a cop-out. To cope with and resolve problems, we must *attend* to them.

Many of these strategies go along with the win-lose approach. The goal is to "win" by proving that I am right and you are wrong. Yet no one likes to lose; no one likes to be made wrong. An emotionally charged power struggle ensues and often escalates. Self-esteem is at stake: "If I don't win, I'm not okay; therefore I must win." The problem may appear to be settled, but it isn't because the loser is angry and resentful. No one comes out winning.

When facing a problem, it helps to examine the underlying goal. Do you want to "win" at the other's expense? Or do you want to resolve it to everyone's satisfaction?

It *is* possible to solve problems with no one losing. Win-win problem solving calls for direct, honest, and assertive communication and willingness to really listen and understand each other. It takes time, energy, and self-discipline. Both people get their needs met.

The goal of win-win strategies is to resolve the problem so that both parties are satisfied. The focus is not on the persons but on the solution—"What will we *do* about it?" The underlying attitude is respect—for oneself and for the other. Both must accept responsibility for the problem and be committed to resolving it without damaging the relationship.

Win-win solutions take time, energy, and self-discipline. Sometimes we have to bite our tongues so they don't get us into trouble. This approach is not easy, but it's worth it. Increased respect, intimacy, and enhanced self-esteem are the payoff.

Stepping-Stones to Problem Solving

- Determine ownership—whose problem is it? Everyone is responsible for solving his or her own problems. Don't solve kids' problems for them unless they are in danger.
- Believe that your problem is solvable. Be positive, hopeful, and expect good things to come of it.
- Don't try to figure out who's right and who's wrong.
- Evaluate the importance of the problem. Tell how important it is. "This isn't very important, but I'd like to talk about it" or "This is very important to me!"
- Speak in terms of "I want," "I feel" rather than "You did this" or "You didn't do that." The I-statement model (see Chapter 7) often resolves problem situations.
- Express your beliefs, values, and opinions as your point of view, not as the Truth.
- Feelings are important; listen to them.
- Read between the lines. Try to figure out what's going on underneath the words—fear? anger? a power struggle? protection?—and address that.
- Use active listening skills. (see Chapter 4.) Try to understand their point of view, their way of seeing it.
- Timing is important. Use good judgment as to when to talk, if you are unsure, ask, "Is this a good time to talk?" Allow enough time for discussion.
- Respond to the other; don't react.
- State clearly what you are asking. "I just want you to listen while I tell you what I feel."
- Be willing to make necessary changes.
- Take time out if things get tense. Take a break to cool down. Do something physical to release the tension. Return to problem solving later.
- Check out all assumptions. "Do you mean _____?" "Are you saying _____?"
- Look for the lesson behind the problem.
- Keep focused in the here and now; pulling up ancient history muddles things.
- Forgive others their mistakes and ask forgiveness for your own.
- Try to keep a sense of humor—especially laughing at yourself.
- Rule out violence. It does not solve conflicts and always has negative consequences.
- Get help—family mediation or counseling—if you're having

trouble resolving a problem or if you're having problems with a toddler.

Problem-Solving Model

"You may not be responsible for being down.
but you are responsible for getting up."
—Jesse Jackson[2]

1. **Identify and define the problem or conflict.** What is really the problem? What exactly is wrong? Identify the problem without blaming. Be aware of everyone's feelings and needs.
2. **Brainstorm for possible solutions.** Express and record all ideas as fast as you think of them. Sometimes the craziest, wildest ideas become the best with a little fixing up. No judgment or discussion is allowed while brainstorming.
3. **Evaluate the alternatives.** Look at the consequences of each choice. Would it solve the problem or make it worse? Work together to find a solution acceptable to both parties. Give and take is necessary for a win-win solution.
4. **Choose the best solution.** Both parties need to find and agree to this solution. Both must be committed to doing it.
5. **Implement the solution.** What changes need to be made? Who will do what? When will they do it? For how long? It may help to informally write out an agreement and sign it to avoid confusion. Decide when to evaluate how it's working.
6. **Follow-up evaluation.** Assess the results. Is the situation better, worse, or the same? If it is better, do you want to extend the contract? If worse, look for another solution from the brainstorming session and implement it. Be persistent until the problem is resolved.

When we know that we can get through conflicts without losing, we have no need to avoid or withdraw from them. When we acquire skills and experience in resolving touchy situations, our confidence grows, as does our self-esteem. And the more we learn, the more we have to teach our children.

Chapter Fourteen

Touch

"Emotional CPR: one hug, one deep breath. Repeat."[1]

Touch is vital to life. Virginia Satir states that the recommended daily requirement for hugs is: four per day for survival, eight per day for maintenance, and twelve per day for growth. We need to be caressed, cuddled, and stroked as much as we need food. Babies who are deprived of touch can actually die: lacking stimulation and nurturance, their spines shrivel up.

A scientist from the National Institutes of Health claims that lack of touch and pleasure during the formative years of life is the principal cause of human violence. He claims that individuals and societies that experience and promote physical pleasure are also peaceful societies. "As either violence or pleasure goes up, the other goes down," states J. W. Prescott.[2]

Many people suffer from touch disorders: from neglect (insufficient touch), from battering (painful touch of the wrong strength), and from incest (inappropriate, violating touch). Touch can be a cruel and damaging violation of another person, or it can be a nourishing gift of love and pleasure that we give to those we care for. The choice is ours.

For persons who have been abused, it seems that the necessary healing for that damage should come through the same modality. If, for example, the abuse was verbal, then positive, loving words can be very healing. If the abuse was physical, healing can be facilitated through respectful, appropriate, loving touch.

We learned about touch from our parents. If they cuddled and hugged us a lot, we learned to enjoy touch. If they touched us mostly in punishment and abuse, we probably learned to fear and avoid touch. This fear is also reinforced by the violent touch seen in the media.

We learn from the media that touch is often sexual. Yet sexual touch is only one type of touch. Most touch is warm, affectionate, and nonsexual. We must understand this, unravel the confusion, and separate the two in our minds. We need to re-learn touch as affection which expresses caring.

In New Zealand some nurses work with a group of parents who are at risk of abusing their children because abusive touch was the only touch they had learned. Every week they attend a lecture on childrearing, have a cup of tea, and do the following exercise to learn how to touch in a healthy, loving way.[3] Try this variation, called "Weather Report," on your spouse or on a child. (The person receiving this attention is in charge and should give feedback.)

Snowflakes. Tap fingertips rapidly and lightly on the head, shoulders, and back.

Raindrops. Tap fingertips simultaneously and with greater intensity.

Thunderclaps. With cupped palms, clap hands across the back and shoulders.

Eye of the tornado. Put your hands on the person's shoulders and circle your thumbs down either side of the spine and across the shoulders.

Tidal wave. Slide your hands in long strokes up and down the arms and across the back.

Calm after the storm.[4] Rest your hands on their shoulders for a few moments. Then hold them one half-inch above for a few moments. Then step back.

One New Zealand mother reported that she wanted to hit her baby but massaged his back instead. The parents at my workshops loved it! One mother reported that her child had difficulty getting to sleep. She tried this and, she said, "he turned into jello and was out." It's a fun and relaxing gift to give. Everyone's self-esteem goes up.

Child Abuse
"Those who cannot remember the past are condemned to repeat it."
—George Santayana[5]

Physical, emotional, verbal, and sexual abuse create enormous problems and pain for individuals, families, and all of society. They damage self-esteem and mental health. They destroy trust. We don't want to hear about them. We don't want to—or are afraid to—talk about them. Yet we must discuss them in order to break the cycle of violence.

Sexual child abuse refers to any inappropriate sexual exposure or touch between an adult and a child. It is inappropriate because the child does not understand the nature of the request and/or because the child is coerced through threats or deceit—that is, that this is "normal" affection. It is inappropriate because an adult takes advantage of a child's innocence, needs, or fears. It is highly damaging to the child and to the relationship.[6]

Overly severe physical punishment—hitting, pinching, burning—has caused unspeakable harm and widespread societal violence. It's not right for people who say they love you to hurt you in the name of discipline. Corporal punishment and neglect can lead to psychopathology in children and misery in families.

Authorities estimate that in our country up to 90 percent of murders, rapes, and other violent crimes are committed by people who were child-abuse victims. Adolf Hitler, Charles Manson, and Lee Harvey Oswald—to name but three—were all victims of child abuse.

Behavioral patterns are handed down from one generation to the next. Rejected children tend to become rejecting parents; abused children become abusive parents. The patterns tend to repeat—generation after generation—*if we let them.*

Many people don't recognize that their primary role models were negative, and therefore they don't see the negative patterns they are following until harm has been done. In continuing the habits and repeating the same old mistakes, they become negative models for their own children, and the pattern repeats for yet another generation.

As people begin to recognize their patterns, they gain the freedom to choose differently. *With awareness comes choice.* With determination and support from others (perhaps professional therapists), a negative situation can be turned around.

When battering occurs in families, many of the following traits may be present in the parents. (Some of them may be present without battering).

• **Distorted view of the child.** Parents may believe that a child is basically bad and deserving of punishment. (See Chapter 15.) They may rationalize abusive treatment, claiming it is necessary to prevent evil behavior from developing.

• **Unrealistic expectations.** "From early infancy, children of abusing parents are expected to be submissive, respectful, thoughtful and considerate of their parents. It is axiomatic to the child beater that infants and children exist primarily to satisfy parental needs, that children's needs are unimportant and should be disregarded, and that children who do not fulfill these requirements deserve punishment,"[7] according to Dr. Brandt F. Steele, chief psychiatrist at the National Center for the Prevention and Treatment of Child Abuse.

Parents may have expectations of the child—and perhaps of themselves—that are too high or impossible. (See Chapter 17.) They don't realize that children are immature. Babies and young children are not always respectful and considerate of their parents. Kids cannot be expected to understand things like adults or to behave like adults. These parents may expect behavior that is developmentally impossible for the child. A five-month-old, for example, cannot be potty trained. Parents may inflict severe punishment for minimal infractions.

• **Warmth is lacking.** Parents may be unaware, unable, or unwilling to relate to and meet their child's emotional needs. Mom may have felt unloved; she may have married for love but found aloneness instead. After a while the child may give up hope of acceptance and love.

• **Parents want the child to fill their needs.** For example, a parent wants the child to love him or her as a parent would love a child. Yet it is impossible for children to do that! Parents who were not loved as children need to fill this need themselves—learning self-love, self-nurturing, and self-care—and get it from loving adults. (See Chapter

18.) Kids do not exist to satisfy their parents' needs. Parents, however, do exist to satisfy their children's.

• **There is a history of battering.** They have learned that beating is the "right way" to discipline children. They are quick to anger and have poor impulse control. They were wounded in their own childhood and are making their children suffer because of it.

• **The focus is negative.** The parent seldom notices or mentions any good qualities in the children but rather is always catching them at being bad. Regardless of the child's efforts to please, the parent may still criticize. The child seldom receives praise.

• **The family is isolated in the community.** The battering family has few close friends, family supports, or social activities. They feel alienated.

• **The parents do not communicate well with their children.** Parents often lack empathy with their children. They do not see things from their child's point of view; they don't put themselves in their child's place. (See Chapter 4.)

• **The parents are likely to withhold privilege and love or isolate a child.** This is probably what their parents did to them. (See Chapter 11.)

• **The parents may not like the child.** They probably don't like themselves, either. Everyone has low self-esteem.

• **The parents believe children must be taught "Who is boss."** Abusive parents believe that children should not be allowed to get away with anything. They are righteous about discipline and punishment. (See Chapter 10.) This attitude (and the other characteristics discussed) may also lead to spouse battering.

• **The parents may imagine that the child is trying to anger or hurt them.** The parents may take things personally that were not meant that way. Kids mostly do things for themselves, not against others.

Finally, the parents may be afraid of hurting or killing the child. Once this is admitted, a turning point has been reached. Immediate action should be taken. Call a mental health professional.

Each year thousands of children are paralyzed, physically deformed, mentally damaged and killed through abuse. There is a direct cause-effect relationship. When abuse occurs, damage results. Many parents don't realize how fragile a child's body is. Striking a child's body is dangerous. One slap on the cheek of a small child can bruise the brain and cause permanent retardation. A sharp yank of the arm can dislocate it. Parents must learn to control damaging impulses. Take time out to cool off. Get away from the dangerous situation. Ask for help. Call the national toll-free number for ChildHelp, a crisis/referral line: 1-800-422-4453.

Parents can also get into trouble if they fail to realize that children have a different time sense. For a young child, ten minutes is almost forever! If you sit a child in the corner for an hour, that's abuse. There are better ways to discipline children. (See Chapter 11.)

People don't generally wake up in the morning saying, "I think I'll whomp my kid today." As the day goes on and stress builds, something or someone "pushes a button" that "triggers" them, and they react. It is important to learn about your buttons and triggers—and how to defuse them. What happened just before you "lost it"? Magnify that moment; unravel it. What can you do to prevent it from happening again? If you need help doing this, get it.

I remember a time many years ago when I got very angry about a mess in the living room. In trying to figure out why I got so angry, I realized that I thought I had to be a "perfect" housewife in order to feel okay. I saw the mess as a sabotage of my struggle for perfection—of my attempt to be okay. Giving this a great deal of thought, I decided that I did not really believe in or want those impossible standards that I'd been trying to live up to, but I *did* want to feel good about myself and my kids. I eased my standards of cleanliness to allow everyone to be more comfortable, relaxed, and happy. I also discovered other ways to develop my self-esteem.

Our parents raised us the only way they knew how, and we learned to parent from them. Remember not only what they did to you but also its effect on you and on your relationship with your parents. Remember how it affected your self-esteem.

Our parents made mistakes. Everyone makes mistakes. Blaming only gets us stuck. It's healthier to forgive them. *Learn from their mistakes, don't repeat them.* Create the future you deserve and desire for yourself and your family. *Only you can change the course of your personal history.* You have the power to do it. If you need help, get it.

A friend of mine shared her story:

A battered child myself, I had no awareness of the incredible anger stored inside me until a month or so after my daughter was born. Having been raised with impatience, demands, and punishments, my instinctual behavior was to lash out whenever her needs conflicted with my limits. While in my mind I saw only love for her, I continued to hurt the most precious being in my life.

When she was one and a half, I made a conscious commitment to become the person I knew I could be, which brought me, two years later, to the realization that violation and violence had been passed down the line of women in our family, and that if I did not stop the pattern, the battering tendency would continue with my daughter. I took responsibility for making that change.

It's now been twenty years, and we have created a loving, accepting, respectful, and caring relationship. A long time coming, it has definitely been worth the effort.

You can break the cycle of violence and create a cycle of love. It all begins with you.

> *"Love is the answer, whatever the question."*
> —A Course in Miracles[8]

Chapter Fifteen

Beliefs

"Whether you believe you can or believe you can't, you're right."
—Henry Ford[1]

The beliefs people hold to be true deeply and profoundly affect who they are and what they get out of life. What you believe is what you get.

Spend some quiet time with yourself. Allow your beliefs to come into your consciousness much as bubbles rise to the surface of a pond. Take as much time as you need to play with the following list. This is a very important exercise. Write down for yourself your beliefs about

- life
- kids (about teenagers if your kids are older)
- discipline
- being a "good" mom or dad
- yourself
- love

We drag the past with us through our beliefs, expectations, attitudes, and self-talk. All these factors combine to create our reality. This is how it works.

1. **Beliefs.** Your unconscious will believe anything you tell it. You talk yourself into your beliefs, which become your truth. Your unconscious, then, does anything and everything it can to make *your* truth come true. Look at the list of your beliefs. Do you want them to come true? Do they enhance your life? If not, mark them on your paper so you can rethink them and possibly get rid of them. Your beliefs create your expectations.
2. **Expectations.** Once you believe something, you fully expect that's how it will be. Expectations are the most powerful forces in human relations. They become a yardstick by which we measure our children. Impossible expectations (which perfectionists have) are among the most damaging forces there are; that's where parents

make the most errors. (See Chapter 17.) When you expect more than your child can do, you are constantly disappointed and your child is constantly discouraged. Your child doesn't see that the expectation is unrealistic, but concludes, *"I'm* inadequate; something's wrong with *me."* Everyone's self-esteem suffers. Your expectations create your attitudes.

3. **Attitudes.** Attitudes are habits of thought. First we form habits; then habits form us. Attitudes of respect or disrespect, trust or distrust, encouragement or discouragement, love or hate are expressed verbally through our self-talk.

4. **Self-Talk** (thinking). Our words enhance or damage our self-esteem and the self-esteem of others. Words have great creative power. When I think "My kids are neat," I feel gratitude and joy and want to hug them. Their self-esteem is enhanced, and so is mine. Thoughts create feelings and lead to behavior.

5. **Behavior.** We behave as if our beliefs are true. Our reality, therefore, is a result of our beliefs. In order to change behavior, we need to explore the beliefs that underpin the system. To change behavior, we must change the words (self-talk) that precede them.

People have a variety of beliefs about life—for example, "Life is a bowl of cherries," or "Life is the pits." Life is to be enjoyed—or endured. You can't have everything, or you can have it all. Some beliefs are life enhancing. Others create limitations, pain, and havoc in our lives.

Two beliefs about kids are that kids are good and that kids are bad. If I believe that kids are bad, I expect them to misbehave. Irritation, anger, and readiness to use punishment reflect in my attitude. When they do something "bad" I say, "It's just like you to do that," and I reinforce the negative behavior. The kid says to himself or herself in self-talk, "Mom expects me to be a holy terror"—so the kid becomes a holy terror! The kid doesn't want to disappoint me!

Now, there is a very important hook here. We look for things that prove we're right, that fit and validate our beliefs. It's called selective perception.

If I believe that kids are bad, I look for things that prove I'm right. And whatever I look for, I find. In focusing on the negative, I filter out all the fun and delightful things they do. When they are helpful and do cute things, I say, "That's not like you," because it doesn't fit what I believe about them. When their behavior fits my belief, I say, "That's just like you." So for better or worse, I keep reinforcing the behavior that proves that I'm right. Kids repeat the behavior that we reinforce and expect. They become what we believe that they are. *What we believe is what we get.*

Another important hook is, We would rather be right than happy. For example, Dad might say to Jack, "You're no good, just like your Uncle Harry." The label creates a negative expectation that Jack wants to "live up to." A self-fulfilling prophecy, Jack will tend to become like his uncle. Dad feels smug because he was "right" about the kid. Yet everyone is miserable.

Examine your other beliefs. What do you believe about yourself? Self-esteem is believing that you are a worthwhile person. The higher your self-esteem, the higher your expectations (short of expecting "perfection"); the lower your self-esteem, the lower your expectations. And you get in life what you believe you deserve.

Most of our beliefs are beyond our awareness. They were handed down from parents, teachers, television, and the culture in general. Unquestioned, they become our truth. These beliefs, then, comprise our "life program" which we act out on a day-to-day basis.

When something isn't working in their lives, seldom do people search for the real source of the problem and unravel the underlying cause. Yet this is what we must do with the beliefs that limit our lives and harm relationships. We must examine the hand-me-down beliefs, keep those that enhance our lives and our families, and get rid of those that are damaging to ourselves and others. Our beliefs drive the system and create our reality.

> *"As you believe, so shall it be done unto you."*
> —Jesus Christ

The Power of Expectations

Daddy expects me to be grown up.
If I prove to him that I am grown up,
he will love me.
But I feel frightened
because I am just a little kid.
And I feel terrified that he will
find out that I am frightened
and not grown up
and will not love me.
So I pretend not to be terrified
and he is proud of my being
what I am not.
Now he thinks that I am grown up
and I breathe a sight of relief.
But now that I am who I am not,
he expects me to be ever more of who
I am not which terrifies me all the more

because I am now expected to be more of
someone I never was.
To complicate matters, he says I should never lie.
So if I tell him that I am not grown up,
he will be proud of my telling him the truth.
But I can not tell the truth
about not telling the truth
because that is admitting to a lie.
Therefore, I must try harder
to be who I am not.[2]

—Anonymous

Chapter Sixteen

Self-Talk

"All that we are is the result of what we have thought."

—Buddha

Several years ago I had an experience that helped me understand self-talk. I used to stalk wild asparagus in the spring. Equipped with a pillowcase and a tiny pocket knife, I set out every four or five days looking for new shoots. One beautiful day, I discovered some luscious stalks just begging to be picked—on the wrong side of a barbed-wire fence. I tried to resist the temptation, but . . .

While harvesting my new asparagus patch, I became aware of someone approaching me. Turning, I saw an older man carrying a little brown bag—and a great big butcher knife! I stood, smiled weakly, and gulped. He said his name was Mr. Miller and mumbled something about "territory," which made me a little nervous. Wanting to change the subject, I asked him to tell me a little about himself. He had grown up there, and as a kid used to ice skate for miles on the frozen ditch. In an effort to make a graceful exit before he could bring up territory again, I invited him to join my family for a steak and asparagus dinner. He smiled and said, "Much obliged ma'am, but I don't mix well."

His words echoed in my mind as I walked home. Mr. Miller had probably said "I don't mix well" thousands, if not millions, of times throughout his life—to himself and to others. People always project self-talk.

Our *self-talk* creates our *feelings*, which express themselves through our actions or *behavior* and become the basis of our *self-concept*.

1. **Self-concept.** Many people have a mistaken idea of self-concept, or self-image. Janet might say, "I was shy when I was born, I'm shy today, and I'll be shy the day I die." Janet is stuck. Self-concept is simply the picture, opinion, or judgment you have of yourself at any given moment.
   Self-image is what you imagine about yourself. Your self-image determines your performance. Self-concept changes as you change. A negative self-image automatically sets up a failure mechanism. A positive self-image sets up a success mechanism.

2. **Self-talk.** This refers to the running commentary we make on everything in our lives. We talk to ourselves all of the time. Self-talk is the most important and powerful voice we hear. Self-talk determines our self-esteem. The reason most people have low self-esteem is that they keep telling themselves how awful they are. This is called "stinkin' thinkin'."

   With our self-talk, we constantly lift ourselves up or put ourselves down. We are our own best friend or our own worst enemy. Only when we tune in and listen to it can we change it. *With awareness comes choice.* Start listening to your internal monologue. Do you like what you hear? What would you do if someone else said those things to you?

3. **Feelings.** Our self-talk, for better or worse, affects our emotions. Imagine yourself saying over and over, "I'm a failure." As you worry that you might fail, you create feelings of failure: discouragement, defeat, and depression. Now, let that go. Say to yourself several times instead, "I'm a winner." Your thoughts about winning and succeeding create winning feelings: encouragement, support, motivation, and excitement.

4. **Behavior.** Our feelings express themselves in our behavior or actions. If we feel like winners, we act like winners—working hard, thinking clearly, and doing what we need to do to win. If we feel like losers, we will act like losers and become losers. Our behaviors reinforce our self-concept—seeing ourselves as either winners or losers.

Let's apply this model to Mr. Miller. His self-talk was "I don't mix well." If you repeated that over and over to yourself, what would you feel? Lonely, lacking in confidence, low in self-esteem? How would you behave? Might you be socially awkward, withdrawing, isolated? Having never married, Mr. Miller lived alone at the edge of town. He carried a large knife and turned down invitations for steak and asparagus dinners. Behavior creates and reinforces self-concept; he probably sees himself as shy—perhaps as a social misfit. This ties in to his self-talk, his feelings, his behavior, and his self-concept. This whole behavior pattern may have begun years ago. Perhaps he overheard an off-hand remark from a significant person. He internalized it and keeps replaying it in his self-talk.

I once heard of a woman who cried herself to sleep every night because she thought she was a "bad" mother. That thought created feelings (guilt, sadness, and anger) that led to behavior (crying every night) that affected her self-concept. That woman needs to ask herself a lot of questions; e.g., What does it mean to be a "good" or "bad" mother? Who's definition am I using? What specifically is the problem? Who can help me solve it?

If I worked with her in therapy, I would help her explore those questions. I would ask her to think about a time when she thought she was a "good" mom. She might tell me about cuddling her child as she put him to bed. Then I'd ask her to tell me about another time, and another. I'm certain that there have been many times that she was a "good" mom, but with her negative belief (selective perception) she had not noticed them. She looked only for situations that fit her belief and proved that she was right, and she didn't see or remember all the good times.

I'd invite her to change her self-talk. On a three-by-five card, I would write, "I, Patricia, am a good mom," and I'd tell her to say that over and over again, twenty to thirty times every day until she believed it, until she became it.

If you were to say to yourself over and over, "I'm a good mom/dad," what would you feel? You would probably feel better about yourself, less stressed, more accepting, and more confident. You'd feel encouraged by the self-talk and positive feelings and would be motivated to behave accordingly. Over time, we tend to become what we think about the most.

I'd like to ask you to pause and do a little fantasy. Imagine, for a minute, a blue hippo. Then,—*don't* think of a blue hippo!

How did you get rid of the blue hippo? You probably thought of something else—maybe a red hippo or a green giraffe or a flower. To get rid of the first image, most people replace it with another. And that is exactly how we must work with our unconscious to make important changes in our lives. Think about what you *do* want in order to get rid of what you *don't* want.

For better or worse, we talk ourselves into everything before we do it. We need to give ourselves messages that affirm the positive in our lives and help bring it about. Affirmations empower us to change our thinking—and our lives.

Affirmations help us believe in the good things we want and expect for ourselves. With commitment and discipline, we can substitute positive messages to expel the garbage from our minds and to heal the damage caused by years of negative thinking. Affirmations are a way to reprogram ourselves and create the kind of transformation we felt when we learned to ride a bicycle or swim. We can move from "I can't" to "Of course I can!" We no longer have to be controlled by our past.

97

I'd like to invite you to do another fantasy. Close your eyes and imagine someone very special entering the room, walking up behind you, gently touching your shoulders, and whispering something that you've been wanting to hear.

These whispered words may be the perfect affirmation for you. Rephrase them in the form, "I _____, am _____." Repeat the affirmation twenty to thirty times every day, allowing the positive feelings— until you believe it, until you become it. You can be your own best friend and give this message to yourself instead of hoping and wishing for someone else to say it for you.

This process makes more sense once you understand the nature of the unconscious: it can't tell the difference between fact and nonfact, between what's imagined and what's real. Your unconscious will believe anything you tell it and will do everything to make that happen. As with a fertile garden, whatever you plant in your unconscious will grow. If you plant carrots, you won't get petunias; and if you plant nothing, you'll probably get weeds.

What are the seeds for the unconscious? The thoughts we think (self-talk) and the pictures we imagine. "Imagination is everything," said Albert Einstein. "It is the preview of life's coming attractions." What we see is what we get. Also, the words we repeat over and over in our minds have great power; eventually they become our reality. *We become what we think about the most.*

We *can* direct our thoughts. When we accept responsibility for our self-talk we come to see that positive thoughts lead to positive self-esteem, and negative thoughts to negative self-esteem. By taking charge of our self-talk we can change our self-esteem. *By changing our minds, we can change our lives.*

One tool for making changes is the use of *turnabout statements*. With our words we can either lock ourselves into old, unwanted behaviors, or we can free ourselves to make new choices for the future. For example:

> "In the past I was closed to new ideas, but now my mind is open."
> "I used to believe that I could never _____, but now I know that I can do anything I want."
> "I used to think that _____, but now I realize _____."
> "Up until now _____."

When children state they can't do something, say, "Let's pretend that you can!" And be sure to read that wonderful story *The Little Engine That Could*. That little engine knew how to use positive self-talk to achieve greatness.

I think I can
I think I can
I think
   I can

Turnabout phrases release us from the undesired, habitual behavior of the past and encourage us to begin new, healthier behavior.

Let's look again at the model.

SELF-CONCEPT→SELF-TALK→FEELINGS→BEHAVIOR

A child with a positive self-concept and high self-esteem is a child who will have positive behavior that reinforces the positive self-concept. On the other hand, a child with a negative self-concept and low self-esteem will exhibit negative behavior that reinforces the negative self-concept. Whatever you can do to build your child's self-esteem will pay off in a happier child with more positive behaviors.

One of the best things you can do for the health and self-esteem of your child is to enhance your own health and self-esteem. Children learn from example—they imitate you. As you enhance and improve your own life, you are providing a model for theirs.

Chapter Seventeen

Perfectionism

"There is no perfectionism. It's really the world's greatest con game;
it promises richness and delivers misery. . . .
So if you are a perfectionist, you are
guaranteed to be a loser in whatever you do."
—David Burns, M.D.[1]

Self-esteem is as important to our well-being as legs are to a table. It is essential for physical and mental health and happiness. Given its importance, everyone should be taught self-esteem development skills—for themselves and for their families. Instead, we are more often taught ideas and behaviors that lower self-esteem—our own and that of our children.

There are many cultural barriers to high self-esteem and mental health. Chapters 17 and 18 identify some of these barriers and offer positive alternatives.

Perfectionism

A perfectionist is someone who is always looking for something wrong, finds it of course (because you always find what you're looking for), and then is shocked and angry about it. Perfectionism has reached epidemic proportions. About 99 percent of my workshop participants either are themselves perfectionists, have lived or worked with perfectionists, or were raised by perfectionists. Perfectionism is very hard on self-esteem, for adults and for children alike.

Think about those people who are perfectionists. What are they like? Take a moment to write down some of their characteristics and how they affect others.

Get in touch, also, with your own feelings about perfectionists. Are you comfortable being around them? Are they fun to be with? Do you want to invite them to your home?

Perfectionists have unrealistic or impossible expectations: only perfection will do. Yet human beings can't be perfect for very long. With one failing, fault, or flaw, a perfectionist thinks she's a total failure who deserves to suffer. This either/or thinking allows no middle ground. As one woman learned clearly from her mother, "You are perfect, or you are nothing." Mistakes, therefore, are terrifying.

Since little in life is perfect, perfectionists are frequently frustrated, disappointed, and angry. It is very difficult for them to accept themselves—or others—as they are. They are very critical and judgmental: no one is good enough. At the same time, they fear criticism and easily become defensive; they can't stand the thought of being wrong. This can result in conflicts in family and professional relationships.

Striving to be "perfect" creates pressures and problems. It is, for example, very difficult to make a "perfect" decision; decision making, therefore, produces anxiety. Perfectionists procrastinate in doing tasks or don't finish them. Sometimes they don't try at all; if they don't try, they reason, they can't fail. Or they may do all the work themselves because no one else can do it well enough.

Perfectionism has an external focus. The emphasis is on surface qualities—for example, what they do, what they have, what they know, how they perform, how they look. Under the influence of perfectionistic thinking, they focus on developing a "perfect" superficial (false) self, based on an image/ideal/fantasy of how they think they are "supposed" to be, in hopes of impressing and pleasing others. Less attention is given to important inner qualities of the real self, to who they most honestly are.

It's very hard work to be a perfectionist! One mother of three little children, for example, vacuumed her carpets three times a day. If she ever achieved "perfection," it didn't last very long. Once the carpet collected a piece of fuzz, it was all over. After discussing this in my workshop, she made some changes; she vacuumed only once each day. She reported having more time to be with the kids—and no one even noticed that she'd cut back.

Nothing is ever good enough for a perfectionist. No one is ever good enough. Perfectionists can achieve great successes yet feel like failures. Always finding something wrong, they never appreciate or celebrate their wins because they know that they could have done better. If a fund raiser brought in $20 million for United Way, a perfectionist would put himself down for not having raised more. This cruel self-talk robs any success of its sweetness.

Perfectionism is a compulsion that creates stress and suffering and makes spontaneity and playfulness rare. Fun and joy are lacking in "perfect" lives. The pressures of perfectionistic thinking may predispose people to alcoholism, eating disorders, and other obsessive-compulsive behaviors. Perfectionists wear blinders: they have a very narrow focus on minute (negative) details and miss the big picture (and the good) entirely.

I am a recovering perfectionist. I remember how hard it was, how frustrating and self-defeating. Since I discovered that I don't have to be perfect to be okay, life has been easier, better, and much more fun. Life can be great if you don't expect it to be perfect.

The Alternative

Perfectionism is deadly, both psychologically and physiologically. Child perfectionists can get A's for twelve years, then get one B and kill themselves. What a tragedy!

As children many of us concluded that only if we were "perfect" would our parents love us. Having to earn acceptance and love, we tried harder and harder to be accepted, to be loved, to be okay. This distorted thinking became internalized, creating an ongoing struggle for perfection in the hope that Mom and Dad might accept, approve, and love us unconditionally—just for being ourselves.

The media, Hollywood, and ladies' magazines urge us to become a "perfect wife," a "perfect mother" of "perfect children," a "perfect body," a "perfect gourmet cook," and so on. Only if we are "perfect" do we think we are okay.

Yet there is no such thing as a "perfect parent," a "perfect child," a "perfect husband and wife," or a "perfect family." No human being is perfect. When under that pressure, we pretend, cover up, or manipulate to keep up a facade. Playing a role while knowing inside that it's phony creates even more stress.

Everyone makes mistakes. As human beings we sometimes fall, forget, spill, and lose things. And that's okay. *It is our privilege as human beings to be imperfect!* It takes courage to allow ourselves to be imperfect and to accept our humanness.

Mistakes terrify perfectionists. Yet *the only people who never make mistakes are those who never do anything*. In filmmaking, actors make mistakes all the time. What do they do with a mistake? They cut it—then do a retake! Afterward they show it to the world so everyone can get a good laugh from the bloopers.

From filmmakers we can learn what to do with our mistakes: cut (stop) and do a retake. We need to fix the mistake and learn from it. There is no need for guilt. We need to forgive ourselves, laugh at it, and go on.

Liz told about her ten-year-old daughter Amanda who received a call from a friend who was upset about receiving an F on a school paper. Amanda gently assured her that she was not her grade and that she was a wonderful friend. Amanda also told her that her F simply meant that she had more things yet to learn.

Children are very human. They are always losing, forgetting, or spilling things. And that's okay! Those are just mistakes. Help them turn mistakes into teachers. Help them figure out what happened and what they can learn to avoid a repeat performance. A mistake, after all, is just one way that didn't work. You might say, "That's not like you; you're better than that."

Children's self-esteem drops when they make mistakes; encourage them to fix the mistake, and their self-esteem will go up. Don't cry over spilled milk; just clean it up and learn the lesson. When we learn what we did wrong, we know how to not make the same mistake again. If we don't learn, we are likely to repeat it.

It's also important to admit your own mistakes. Say to your kids, "Yesterday I said (or did) _____ and I realize today that I was wrong." Everyone makes mistakes, and that's okay. It's not okay to make the same mistake over and over again without learning the lesson behind it.

Look for the humor in your personal bloopers. Share them around the dinner table. One mom told me that they play Bloopers at dinner. Mom and Dad begin, and each kid follows. It's a relief not to have to be perfect, not to have to play God. As one parent moaned, "Where is it written that parents always have to be right?" The burden lightens when you can accept yourself completely—including the fact that you sometimes make mistakes.

In doing, risking, and trying new things, we develop judgment skills. We learn how to evaluate, how to analyze, how to determine what old information transfers to new situations. If it works, we've increased our competence and confidence. If it doesn't work, it's another learning opportunity. A person who has made mistakes has gained wisdom.

We need to accept and forgive ourselves and our children. We must pick ourselves up, brush ourselves off, and figure out how to do it differently next time.

When we understand and accept our humanness, laugh at ourselves, learn the lessons, and forgive ourselves, we gain wonderful skills that will serve us throughout our lives. Modeling this is a wonderful gift to our children.

When people learn from mistakes, they gain competence, confidence, and wisdom. Hopefully, children can learn from little mistakes early in life when they're around people who love them. As they get older, the stakes get higher; many mistakes are lethal.

It can be difficult for parents to watch their kids struggle as a result of their mistakes. The impulse to protect and rescue them is there.

Don't, however, rescue them from their mistakes unless they are in danger. When we rescue them from the consequences of their behavior, they don't learn their lessons. For example, when a child forgets a homework assignment and Mom brings it to school, the child does not learn from that and will probably forget it again. If Mom didn't rescue the child, he or she would experience the consequences, perhaps miss recess to redo the homework, and be more likely to learn a lesson.

It may take them two or three times to learn to not repeat a mistake. Allow for that. When a lesson is learned, let it go; forgive and forget the mistakes—and hope your children do the same for you.

"The only real mistake is the one from which we learn nothing."
—John Powell[2]

Thomas Edison failed two thousand times before he succeeded in inventing the electric filament. Someone once said, "Tom, don't you feel bad about all your mistakes?" He responded, "No, inventing the filament was a two-thousand-and-one-step process!" Each failure gave him important feedback that moved him closer to his big success. One could say that Edison failed his way to success.

The second suggestion for transcending perfectionism addresses the damaging self-talk that says, "I'm not good enough." Try to become aware of whose voice it is that says that to you; then realize that that was only their opinion based on their perfectionist expectations. The fact is, *you are good enough and always have been!*

You need to change the damaging message that keeps telling you differently. Say, instead, "I, [your name], am good enough." Repeat this a few times. It may feel strange, perhaps not true at first, but that will change. As this affirmation begins to feel right, it will heal you and help move you beyond perfectionism.

Third, allow flexibility. Instead of trying to be perfect in everything you do, decide what's really important to you and go for excellence in that area. Be the best that you can be! In other areas, know that you are okay and can be even better—if you want that. With certain things, planting a garden, for example, allow yourself to be "good enough;" beet seeds do not have to be in a straight line exactly one half-inch deep and one half-inch apart! In allowing and encouraging yourself to be flexible, you can stretch to help yourself get beyond the compulsion of having to be perfect in everything you do.

The final suggestion is to put some spontaneity, some silliness, some joy into your life. Your kids can teach you how to play. Roll down a grassy hill with them. Skip rope. Go down a slide. Your self-esteem will go up, and so will theirs. Laughing and playing together will reduce stress, create rich memories, and nudge you beyond perfectionism.

It's hard to be a friend unless you be yourself. It's hard to be your self unless you know yourself. It's hard to know yourself unless you admit mistakes. It's hard to admit mistakes when you're trying to be perfect. And it's hard to try to be perfect—very hard indeed. It's easier to just be honestly who you are: an imperfect yet lovable and okay human being.

Chapter Eighteen

Other Cultural Stumbling Blocks

*"The first problem for all of us, men and women,
is not to learn, but to unlearn."*
—Gloria Steinem[1]

Little children have wonderful memories. They are, by nature, very impressionable because they have so much to learn to prepare themselves for the rest of life.

Children are ready and eager to learn about their world and to learn how to be in it. They are trusting and believe what they are told. They learn from everything. They accept whatever they learn as the "truth" about how the world is. They do as they are told.

In simpler cultures this works very well. From parents and others who care about them, children learn what they need to know in order to become effective adults. In our culture things are different. Children learn less from their busy parents, little from neighbors, and too much from television and Hollywood. As a result, they miss out on essential lifeskills they need to become healthy and competent adults. The mass-media cultural values, and myths clutter their minds with misinformation that can imprison them in pain and grief.

I have spent many years sifting through what I have learned, unraveling the misinformation, poking holes in the myths, peeling off the layers. I had to unlearn what didn't work, then relearn what did. At age forty, I finally knew what I needed to know at fourteen.

In this chapter I discuss other cultural barriers to self-esteem and mental health. They can be deadly—either psychologically (draining our life force), or physically (resulting in suicide). Once we identify the stumbling blocks, we can turn them into stepping-stones for personal growth. Once we see clearly, we can help our children avoid the pitfalls. It is better to prepare than repair.

Not long ago, a popular high school senior—a track star—went home after school, wrote a note to his parents, and left. The note simply said, "I won't be home tonight." He went out and shot himself. In trying to make sense out of it, they discovered that earlier that day he found out he had received a lesser scholarship than his brother. He had compared himself unfavorably, then taken his life.

Comparison

Comparison is a setup for competition and low self-esteem. Did your parents ever compare you with a brother or sister? Did they play favorites? How did you feel when they did that? What were they trying to do? Did it work? Think about your present relationship with that sibling.

Ann told me, "There were four girls in our family. We were often compared to each other in looks, intelligence, athletic ability, and so on. For the most part, I tried to 'hold my own' by competing with my sisters. My youngest sister felt defeated and reacted by not participating at all. Most of my self-esteem problems stem from the fact that I was never as 'wonderful' as my oldest sister."

Comparison inspires interpersonal competitiveness and defeat. My success depends on your failure, and you are hoping that I will fail. This win-lose situation leads to anxiety and loss of self-confidence, which interfere with performance. Comparison also interferes with co-operation and teamwork. No one really wins.

Competitiveness has been considered a national virtue that brings out the best in us. Yet evidence shows that this is not true. In fact, competition may make people suspicious and hostile toward others. They are less apt to trust or communicate with one another. Competition separates people and drives them apart. When we compete and compare ourselves with others, we can always feel like failures because there's someone better than we are.

Do you ever compare yourself with others? With whom? One person? Two? More? What do you do after you compare yourself?

Often we trap ourselves by identifying the best qualities of many different people, synthesizing them into a fantasy ideal, and then trying— as a single human being—to live up to that impossible image. We put others on a pedestal while putting ourselves down, and our self-esteem suffers in the process.

The Alternative

Competition between individuals can be very destructive. Win-lose situations can damage relationships and families. We can let go of the tendency to compete with everyone. We can learn instead to appreciate the differences and be sincerely happy for others' achievements and successes. As one woman stated, "Edna's a good cook, so let her cook!" This shift from win-lose to win-win thinking makes life less stressed and more fun. The win-win belief fosters cooperation, which is essential for winning famlies.

Cooperation is necessary for healthy families and also for success in business. The Apple Computer Corporation began as a backyard operation characterized by intense teamwork. Working and pulling together is the solid foundation on which successful businesses and winning families alike are built.

Comparison encourages and enforces conformity. But you don't have to be like everyone else! As a matter of fact, you *can't* be like everyone else, because you are one of a kind. It's okay to be who you really are. If you aren't you, who will be?

Since the beginning of time, billions of people have inhabited our planet. Yet there has never been anyone like you. You are unique. You are special. You are a divine original. The only person you can really compare yourself with is *you*.

How are you today as compared with three months ago or three years ago? Are you more loving, more accepting? Are you a better person, or are you backsliding? Compare yourself only with you and your own personal growth. Compete only with yourself. Challenge yourself to become your own personal best.

Finally, when you notice that you are comparing yourself to (and competing with) another, change your self-talk. Instead of putting yourself down, consider the other person a model and lift yourself up. "If it were really important to me, I could be as good a speaker as Rita." We are hungry for models. Seeing with new eyes, we can find people everywhere who can inspire us to excellence.

Self Put-Downs

Many people learned that it is not okay to say good things about themselves. When they did, they were criticized for "tooting their own horn," being conceited, or bragging. So they learned to change their self-talk and put themselves down instead. Doing that, their self-esteem suffered.

The Alternative

People do not achieve greatness while telling themselves how awful they are. Scientists and soccer players, mothers and musicians, become great by wanting it, by believing in themselves, and by working for it. After setting a goal, they encourage and support themselves (self-talk) and take pride in their progress.

The word pride is used both positively—"I'm proud of you"—and negatively—"Don't be proud." To me, to be proud means to feel good about someone and/or their performance. On the other hand, to put yourself up and others down—"I'm great and you're not"—is false pride and is negative. It confuses self-estem with power.

Listen to what you say to yourself. Look into a mirror and tune in to your self-talk. How would you feel if a friend talked to you like that? It's okay to whisper "sweet nothings" in your ear. And most other people would really prefer to hear the good things about you and your life rather than the negative things.

Begin also to listen closely to how you talk to your children. Listen for, then ban negativity; it lowers self-esteem. Catching your kids being good and noticing it will make them more aware of their positive attributes and raise their self-esteem.

Listen to how your children talk about themselves. Negative statements, such as "I'm dumb" or "I never do anything right," let you know what they are repeating over and over again to themselves. The negative self-talk leads to negative feelings and negative behavior. (See Chapter 16.)

To counter this, you might introduce the Eleventh Commandment: "Thou shalt not speak negatively of thyself or others." Establish a rule that every negative statement about oneself is to be countered with a positive statement. This will help you become aware of how you talk to yourself—and about others—and will flip the focus to the positive instead.

Try the "Tell Me How You're Terrific" exercise. (See Chapter 2.) Look for the good qualities in yourself and in your kids. Encourage them to look for and talk about how they're special. Parents and teachers alike report that kids love doing this.

Confusing the Person with the Behavior

Did you ever do something stupid? Does that mean that you *are* stupid? Of course not! *What you do is not who you are.*

Remember a time when, as a child, someone pointed a finger at you and yelled, "You're a bad boy" or "You're a bad girl." What did you feel? Did you feel it again just now? How old were you at the time?

One woman stated, "I did a dumb little thing, and with those words my mother wiped me out. Yelling that I was a 'bad girl' devastated me. I felt rejected, worthless, awful, and unlovable. Looking back, I realize that I wasn't a bad girl; I was a good girl who had made a dumb mistake."

Those significant persons probably did not understand the importance of separating the person from the behavior. In dealing with the unacceptable behavior, they rejected the whole child, who felt wounded, worthless, and devastated. It is possible to deal with unacceptable behavior without damaging anyone.

The Alternative

We must separate the person from the behavior. When dealing with problem behavior, treat children with respect and caring. Sit down with them; touch them supportively. Love the doer even when you don't like the deed. Then talk about what happened. Imagine that you can hang the problem behavior on the wall so that both can separate from it and discuss it objectively. What happened? What were they thinking? What are they feeling? What can they learn? How can they fix it? With this strategy the problem can get resolved without the child feeling rejected.

Don't call your children "bad." When labeled bad, they feel bad and behave badly—a self-fulfilling prophecy. They are good kids who may, at times, do "bad" things. Tell your children that they are good. Expect them to be good—not perfect. Encourage and appreciate the behavior you want.

Always Pleasing Others

In the past many people were taught to spend their lives trying to please others. They never said no, because someone might be displeased with or even mad at them. They became people-pleasers, begging for crumbs of approval from others. They smiled a lot, hoping that everyone would like them and enjoy being with them. These people never felt okay and suffered from low self-esteem.

The Alternative

The person most important for you to please is yourself. Think, for a moment, of a time when you prepared a nice meal for someone and worked hard on it but something wasn't quite right. Afterward, someone gave you a compliment—"That was delicious!" What did you do with their remark? Not being pleased yourself, you probably discounted it or ignored it because you didn't believe it. You must first be pleased before you can let in the appreciation and recognition of others. If someone does give you a compliment, it's like icing on a cake.

As a senior in high school, I was voted "the most cheerful" person in a class of three hundred girls. Wanting to be pleasing so that everyone would like me, I wore a permanent smile. It actually had little to do with cheer. I was shocked in graduate school to learn that statistically one out of eight people would not like me (or anyone else).

Struggling with this, I learned that little girls are socialized to want to be liked by others, while boys are socialized to look for respect. I realized that, if being liked is most important, people will do anything to achieve it—even things against their principles. I also realized that it's a vulnerable position, inviting manipulation of others (for example, "If you don't do _____, I won't like you."). Young girls who want to be pleasing to others are easy victims of "date-rape."

After giving this lots of thought, I decided that I would rather have people respect me than like me. I stopped smiling all the time. I began to respect myself more, and others began to respect me more. My self-esteem moved up a few notches.

Assuming Too Much Responsibility for Other People's Lives

When babies are born, parents have total responsibility for their survival and well-being. As they grow and are able to do things for themselves, parents must turn over responsibility to them, thereby lightening their own load.

If this transfer does not occur, if parents carry more responsibility than is necessary or appropriate, children are deprived of opportunities to grow, develop, and expand. Children may not believe that they can take care of themselves or solve their own problems. Then one day, when Mom and Dad aren't around, life will throw them a curve, and, not knowing what to do, they'll probably be overwhelmed.

Parents, carrying too much responsibility, may feel burdened and try to control others. Blame and anger often result with everyone's self-esteem dropping.

The Alternative

Every person is first and foremost responsible for himself or herself. The task of the parent shifts from having total responsibility over infants to having almost no responsibility over them as adults. The task of the child shifts from having no responsibility as an infant to having total responsibility as an adult. This gradual process, in harmony with the developmental stages of the chid, occurs over fifteen to twenty years' time.

We all remember the delight of a youngster saying, "Look at me! I can do it all by myself!" We say, "Good for you! Now you can tie your own shoes." We can release some responsibility.

As children are ready to assume more responsibility for their behavior and their lives, parents can ease up the protectiveness, trust them more, and breathe a sigh of relief as their responsibility lightens. We teach children responsibility by teaching ourselves not to do things for them that they can do for themselves. And as they learn to do more and more things for themselves, their competence and confidence increase.

Alcoholic Family Systems

These are a cause of much pain and low self-esteem. Children of alcoholics are frequently victims of abuse, incest, neglect, and other forms of violence and exploitation. When parents are drunk or high, they may do things they later regret. Many serious and damaging problems go along with alcoholism—emotional, physical, and sexual abuse of children and spouses. Everyone's mental health and self-esteem are damaged.

It's estimated that 28,000 adults grew up with alcoholic parents. They learned certain attitudes and behavior that helped them survive. First and foremost, they learned to deny the problem. They also learned the rules—don't talk, don't trust, and don't feel. The traits that were necessary for survival then get in the way of developing satisfying relationships with family and friends later on in life.

The Alternative

Self-help groups are forming around the country for Adult Children of Alcoholics. These groups—and also AA groups, Al-Anon and Ala-Teen groups—can help you understand the dynamics of alcoholic family systems. They can help people deal with alcoholism, heal themselves, and prevent the disease from recurring in another generation.

Patrick said, "Joining Adult Children of Alcoholics meetings has been the single most helpful and supportive thing I've done in my adult life. For the first time I understand why, for the past thirty-six years, I haven't felt good about myself, why I'm a caretaker and a perfectionist. It's such a relief to be in a roomful of people who accept me as I am, who understand from the inside out what it's like, and to realize that I'm not bad, crazy, or sick—and that it's not hopeless. I've learned that it's okay to take care of myself and to like myself."

If your parents were alcoholic, it's not your fault. You are not responsible for their problems. On the other hand, they may be responsible for some of your problems. But you are the one responsible for the solution to your problems. I strongly encourage you to not deny, but deal with it—for your own sake, and for your kids' sake.

The Win-Lose Approach

The win-lose approach, in which only one person wins and everyone else loses, is hard on self-esteem. Nobody likes to lose, yet mostly we're made to feel like losers. Often, focusing on faults and failures, people talk themselves into becoming losers.

The Alternative

We need to expand our definition of winning. You are a winner. Every success, accomplishment, achievement, every task crossed off a "to do list," is a win! In the grocery store, putting milk into the cart is a win. We are winning all the time. Often, however, our wins go unnoticed and unappreciated by ourselves and others—and our self-esteem sags.

Pause for a moment and make a list of ten wins of the last few days. They can be big or little achievements—for example, getting to work or school on time, asking for something, changing seventeen diapers without complaining, or fixing dinner for the family last night. Now give yourself a big pat on the back. You deserve it because you are a winner.

We all deserve more appreciation. Yet we can't appreciate something if we don't notice it. So we need to start looking for the wins.

When you crawl into bed tonight, don't think of what you didn't finish, what you should have done, what you could have done better. Instead, look for the wins. Every night before you turn off the light, make a list of ten wins, and you'll sleep like a baby. The next day, you will wake up feeling refreshed and positive about life.

You deserve more appreciation. Instead of hoping that maybe someone will notice and appreciate you, *give that to yourself.* You know when you did a good job; tell yourself so. Give yourself a pat on the back.

Appreciation for ourselves and others can turn duty into a gift. It makes us much healthier and more fun to be around. And of course everyone feels better.

"Selflessness"

In the past, many women were taught to take care of everyone else's needs but not their own. They expected and hoped that in doing enough taking care of, their turn would come. They were taught that taking care of themselves was "selfish." They became self-negating; many became martyrs and doormats. "I almost denied myself out of existence," confessed one woman.

Imagine for a moment that you are a pitcher full of love, time, energy, and skills. Now close your eyes and visualize giving of yourself as the pitcher empties. Visualize who then fills your pitcher.

If someone does fill your pitcher for you, consider yourself fortunate. Many women don't get their pitchers filled by others. Many women have not learned to ask for what they want or to teach others how to nourish them. In continuing to give of themselves without replenishment, they have become depleted.

The Alternative

We are responsible for filling our own needs. Everyone has basic human needs that must be filled. These include needs for safety and survival, protection, love, identity, and self-fulfillment. If needs are not met, problems develop. Caregivers have needs that should not be ignored.

"Kids' needs are best met by grownups whose needs are met," writes Jean Illsley-Clarke. Yet there are times when we need to put our own needs on hold, especially with young children. One of the challenges of parenting is to do for our kids *and* for ourselves. We need to strike a healthy balance in which no one comes out losing.

We all need to learn to take care of ourselves. Self-care is the primary issue because we can't give what we haven't got. The last part of the first commandment states that we must love our neighbor *as ourself*. Self-love, therefore, comes first. The best thing you can do for your kids is to be good and loving to yourself.

Exercise

Pause for a moment and make a list of twenty things you love to do. (Be aware, as you are writing, of when the last time that you did those things was.)

Your homework: Every day do at least one of those things for yourself. This is self-nourishment. This is self-care. This is how you can fill your own pitcher.

It has been found that people who are good to themselves feel good about themselves. They then have more love and energy to give to others.

Your intention is important. Most people like to take a hot bath. If you do it because you deserve a treat, because you've earned it, the bath will do more than cleanse you—it will also enhance your self-esteem.

It's okay and necessary for you to take time for yourself. It's also important to take time for your friends, for your spouse. You entered a relationship to be friends, to be lovers, to have fun together. Often, when kids come along, parents fall out of touch with each other. It's important to nurture and enrich your primary relationship; that's where it all started. And one day, when your kids are grown, you will be back to being alone with each other. The love that exists between parents showers down on the children. Being in the presence of two people who truly love and support each other has a powerful positive effect. All relationships need to be nurtured.

Our Bodies are Never Okay

Most women think that something is wrong with their bodies. They compare themselves to the current "perfect" figure, put themselves down, and feel bad. The ideal figure is getting skinnier; the *Playboy* centerfold body is five pounds lighter than she was a few years ago.

The cultural stereotype for women's bodies is not only damaging, it is absurd. In her new book Jane Fonda discusses becoming bulimic in high school. "For several of us at my school," she writes, "it was the beginning of a nightmarish addiction that would undermine our lives for decades to come."[2] Bulimia, anorexia, and other eating disorders have reached epidemic proportions. Little girls nine and ten years old are dieting because their mothers are when they should be having a wonderful time climbing trees, riding bikes, and exploring the world. They have internalized the cultural value that they have to have a "perfect"—skinny—body in order to be okay; they are not okay as they are. Many have learned to hate their bodies and reject themselves.

The Alternative

We come in all sizes, all shapes, all colors—and we are all okay. We need to understand that the cultural model is damaging and unhealthy. Your body is okay. Accept it. Love it just the way it is. If you want to make some changes, you will be more successful by being respectful and encouraging of it than by being rejecting and discouraging of it ("Hey, turkey thighs!").

Sexism and Racism

There are many social injustices that create human distress and pain. We learn, in many ways, that it is not okay to be female—or black, brown, red, yellow, or Jewish. The institutionalized prejudice expressed in unemployment, low-paying menial jobs, and low social status results in victimization, poverty, and poor self-esteem. When we internalize prejudice and social rejection, we turn on ourselves and others like us.

The Alternative

We live in a pluralistic society where all people are created equal. Instead of putting ourselves and others down, we need to lift ourselves and others up. No matter what your race, ethnic origin, sex, or sexual orientation, you are okay. To counter and heal destructive prejudice, affirm your own worth and that of others; e.g., black is beautiful. We have to get rid of mental shackles and join with others for support, healing, strengthening, and working for social change.

Avoidance

Everyone has pain and discomfort at times. What do we learn to do with it?

- Distract ("Let's watch a movie.")
- Deny ("No, no. I'm okay.")
- Drug ("How about a drink?")[3]

For example, I discover a flat tire on my car. If I deny it, distract myself, or have a drink or a pill, the tire is still flat. If I do nothing, nothing changes except my inner experience. If I pretend that it's the way I want it to be, I'm deluding myself.

As long as I keep avoiding, I remain stuck in feelings of helplessness and numbness. When we avoid pain, we hold on to it. It becomes chronic. And it takes more energy to avoid pain than to face it.

The Alternative

Unhappy people and families don't become happy by pretending, denying, or avoiding reality. They become happy by making positive changes. In order for things to change, I must *do* something. I must attend to the flat tire and fix it. In figuring out how to solve a problem, I *do* something, I *change* something, and I *learn* something. When it's resolved, the pain is gone. I am stronger and feel the joy of overcoming. We're put on this earth not to struggle but to grow.

Objectification

Sometimes we don't see people as they really are—as living, changing human beings. Instead, we see them as objects or stereotypes. If I view you as an object, I have a preconceived idea of how you are supposed to be, and I want and expect you to fit the picture in my mind. When you cooperate and are predictable, I am satisfied. If you do not behave the way I think you should, I'll probably be angry and blame you.

Regarding my own actions, those that are consistent with what I want to believe about myself are okay; those that are not are filtered out—denied. Only certain facets of my life, therefore, are accepted. The rest are underdeveloped (frozen) or hidden—from myself and from others.

A simple way to understand this complicated process is to imagine that I have a picture or snapshot in my mind of how I'm supposed to be (the Ideal Me) and one of how you're supposed to be (the Ideal You). You yourself also have an image in your mind of how I'm supposed to be and another of how you're supposed to be. We then want and expect the real person to fit the ideal or "perfect" image.

Any information that is consistent with my mental pictures of myself and you is considered proof that I'm right. Any information that does not fit my picture is filtered out.

In relating to you, I can share only what I share with myself; communication is therefore limited. It is further limited to information that coincides with the image I'm trying to appear to be, or with your image of how you think I ought to be. The rest is concealed—from others and from myself.

Controlling the world to fit the way I think it's supposed to be results in the illusion of stability and predictability. Yet because my perception is narrow and so much is hidden, I will never honestly get to know myself—or you. I will not really see anyone or anything else as they are—but I won't realize that.

Objectification leads to performance ("Smile for the camera"), second-guessing, pretense, stress, and focus on externals. We can spend a lifetime doing what we imagine others want us to do—only to find out that they never really wanted that. We can spend a lifetime never doing what we want, never even knowing what we want, because we're caught up in an imaginary, artificial structure that has little to do with reality.

The Alternative

People are not objects that fit into mental snapshots. They are, rather, like movies—always in motion, always changing, always "in process." People who are really alive and enjoying themselves understand that the snapshot captures certain moments or events. Yet the exciting, vital processes in between—the ups and downs, the ins and outs—give depth and breadth and richness to life.

No one enjoys my photograph albums more than my family because we were there and we remember what happened before and after they were taken. We get excited remembering the whole sequence—the whole process. When I show the pictures to others, they might get an idea of the event, yet only if I fill in the story for them can they get a sense of the excitement and drama that was happening.

Theologian Martin Buber described this concept in terms of an "I-Thou" relationship, as opposed to "I-It" objectification. In the I-Thou approach, mental images and expectations of how people and things are *supposed* to be put aside or suspended. We are instead open to the present moment, to seeing each individual *right now,* without labels, without projections, without the distortion of past memories. We can see how they are changing.

Instead of filtering out—denying—everything that doesn't fit our image, we realize that everything is greater than our present (mis)perception of it. We see the world with new eyes, with a willingness to let in new experiences and information. An attitude of openness follows—toward oneself and others.

It's okay to be who you really are. In fact, it's important, as a parent, that you are first and foremost a real person—yourself. Then look at your kids, beyond the externals. See beyond their appearance, their performance, and their behavior. See the inner beauty and richness that make them unique and lovable.

It's a relief to realize that you don't always have to be on top of things; you don't always have to be strong. You're human—with good and bad days. That's okay. When you accept your own humanness, your kids more readily accept theirs.

This shift brings with it excitement and aliveness; it presents a constantly changing and expanding world. It may also bring some discomfort as the old objectifying, dehumanizing ways thaw out and "the real world" rushes in.

Communication is no longer guarded but is open for learning about and sharing—with oneself and with others. This increases honesty and integrity, freedom, meaningful friendships, and personal growth.

Winning families are made up of such people who see themselves and others as worthwhile persons, not as objects or roles, and who are able to appreciate and understand the exciting inner process of being human.

Faulty Thinking[4]

We learn about ourselves by observing and concluding. Those conclusions become our Truth—even though they may not be true. They can cause difficulty and suffering. Patterns of faulty thinking must be identified and unraveled, understood and changed.

• In **polarized (either-or) thinking,** there is no gray area, no middle ground. You are either good or bad, perfect or a failure. As a result, emotions swing dramatically from one extreme to the other. Because of one little flaw, you become totally worthless. This dangerous, faulty thinking can lead to suicide.

The Alternative. Watch for either-or, black-white judgments. When you catch yourself doing that, ask how the opposite is also true. If, for example, you hear yourself saying, "The house is a total mess," look for parts of the house that are *not* messy. Realize that, with your 1-to-10 thinking, you block out 2, 3, 4, 5, 6, 7, 8, and 9. Look for them. They are there.

• In **personalization** we take everything personally, even when it isn't personal. For example, I might see someone scowling and conclude that she is scowling at me. At dinner, if someone doesn't like broccoli, I might conclude that something's wrong with me and feel hurt.

The Alternative. Don't take it personally if it isn't personal. Check it out. Ask questions. Maybe they just don't like broccoli! Maybe she always scowls! Detach yourself. It doesn't mean anything about you or your personal worth.

We need to look at behavior differently. Mostly, kids and other people are doing things for themselves—not *against* someone else. In some families, there is confusion here. A kid makes a mess, and Mother says, "How could you do that to me?" Well, the kid made the mess for himself or herself, not against Mother. Parents need to separate themselves from their children so they don't take kids' behavior personally. The higher our own self-esteem and the more we learn, the easier it is to not hook in to such things.

• In **mind-reading** we make assumptions about others that are untested and invalid. We project onto others what is going on inside us. We imagine all kinds of awful things and create severe anxiety for ourselves without any basis in reality. A friend, for example, stops in to visit you. You look over your home, noticing how messy it is, and then imagine that he or she is doing the same. You feel bad as a result of what you have imagined and told yourself. It has nothing to do with the other person.

The Alternative. Your negative feelings (guilt, anger, rejection) are the result of your own thinking (self-talk) and probably have nothing to do with your visitor. When you catch yourself mind-reading, try to prove your conclusion. (Is she eyeing everything critically? Is she wearing white gloves? Or is she looking right at you smiling—happy to see you?) Check it out. Chances are it's a fabrication of your own faulty thinking.

• With **catastrophizing** we imagine and expect the worst. A headache is a sure sign of a brain tumor; a minor financial setback means you'll starve to death for sure. Any little thing may be a sign of impending doom.

The Alternative. Consider the odds against your conclusion—the brain tumor, starvation. Don't make a mountain out of a molehill. Realize that those things may be possible but are not very probable.

• In **blaming** we find fault either in ourselves or in others. We either assume total responsibility for everything that goes wrong ("What's wrong with me?") or we accept no personal responsibility for difficulties and put it all on others. We either point a blaming finger at everyone else or beat our breast in guilt.

The Alternative. We are all responsible for our behavior and the consequences of it. In relationships, both persons are responsible for creating the problem—and for creating a solution. Listen for the words "blame" and "fault." Get rid of them. Instead, think in terms of accepting responsibility—and sharing it.

• With **overgeneralization,** if something bad happened to you once, you expect it to happen again. Limited situations lead to absolute conclusions. You make one mistake, and you conclude that you're a "bad" person. Someone else makes a mistake, and you totally reject them. If you notice that one thing is wrong, and another thing, you leap to the conclusion that everything is wrong. You may even talk yourself into believing that it's bad now, it always was, and it always will be—forever and ever, amen.

The Alternative. First of all, be aware of what you are doing. When you notice it, examine the evidence *for* your conclusion and then the evidence *against* it. Weigh your information. Also, listen for those "big" words: never, always, everybody, nobody. Use them only with great care.

• **Having to be right** all the time puts you into conflict with everyone whose viewpoint differs. It makes people hard of hearing. When others differ from you, you ignore them or have to prove them wrong. A power struggle results.

Minor differences seem major because self-esteem and personal worth are at stake. When reality differs from the way you think it should be, you deny it. Having to be right all the time makes people lonely.

The Alternative. Reality is not the way we want it to be—but the way it *is*. We need to remove the blinders and see what really is, instead of trying to force the world to fit our personal image of how it's supposed to be. In our world we have many different people with different perceptions, experiences, and styles. There are many different "right" ways. It would be a dull world if there were only one right way. And whose right way would be accepted as right by everyone else? We must each find what's best for ourselves—what is right—and allow others to do the same.

Positive self-esteem is essential for mental health and happiness. It is a necessary ingredient of a winning family. Yet our culture is very hard on self-esteem, presenting many barriers to mental health and happiness.

We do our best based on the information we have. Yet frequently what we know is incomplete information, or misinformation, or myth. When what we know is incorrect, things don't work out. "I did everything I was supposed to!" I once exclaimed. "Why do I feel so bad?"

Now that you are aware of the barriers, you know what to do. You can unravel the misinformation and poke holes in the myths; you can unlearn what doesn't work and learn what does. Then you can teach the correct information to your kids so they can have their feet on solid ground sooner than you did.

Questions

The questions
Which frighten and make us want to run,
Which evade our socialized minds,
Which have never before been asked—
These are the questions which
We must dare to pursue,
The edges we must explore.

—L. Hart[5]

Chapter Nineteen

Who's Pulling Your Strings?

*"To be nobody but yourself in a world which is doing its best
to make you just like everybody else
means to fight the greatest battle there is or ever will be."*

—e.e. cummings[1]

Everyone has lots of things they have to do. Make a list of five or ten things that you have to, ought to, or are supposed to do. Start each sentence with "I." Then rewrite your list, beginning each sentence instead with "I choose to." Notice the difference you feel.

People do things for two general reasons: to please others and to please themselves. Do you listen more to the external voices—the musts, have tos, ought tos—or do you listen more to your internal voices? Which voices do you respond to?

What you're looking at is your *locus of control,* an awkward phrase that refers to the source or location of the control in your life. If you imagine yourself as an automobile, who is in the driver's seat? In other words, who's in charge? Who's pulling your strings? Who's running your life?

Let's look at the characteristics of people with external and internal centers of control.

Centers of Control

EXTERNAL	INTERNAL
Listens mostly to outside voices ("shoulds," "have to's").	Listens mostly to inner voices ("want to's," "choose to's").
Lives life based on who he or she is supposed to be.	Lives life based on who he or she is.
Avoids personal responsibility; then when something goes wrong, blames others.	Accepts responsibility for himself or herself and for behavior.

Trusts others more than self. Looks to others to take charge, to take care of him or her.	Trusts self more, yet listens to others. Takes charge of own life.
Lacks self-confidence.	Has increasing self-confidence and competence.
Is vulnerable to pressure and manipulation.	Can think and make decisions for himself or herself.
Feels helpless and out of control, like a victim.	Feels in control of life; is pulling own strings.
Worries about what the neighbors think.	Cares more about what he or she thinks; is tuned to inner listening.
Has low self-esteem.	Has high self-esteem

> *"Inner listening makes clearer to us what we really want as distinct from what we have been talked into."*
> —Marilyn Ferguson[2]

When children are little, they have an external locus of control. Parents who know more and have more responsibility usually tell them what to do. As they develop and mature, children learn to think for themselves, trust themselves, and gain in competence and confidence. They learn to stand on their own two feet. There is a natural movement from external to internal centers of control.

For many people, this process has been interrupted or thwarted. There are fifty-year-old people who trust others more than they trust themselves; they have not learned to think independently or become the persons they want to be. They are afraid, for example, to touch the tags on their pillows that say "Do not remove under penalty of law." This is especially common for persons raised in autocratic family systems.

Psychologist Albert Ellis teaches, "Thou shalt not 'should' upon thyself." I did that most of my life. One day, about fifteen years ago, I started to listen to my self-talk. I was very surprised to hear a string of orders bossing me around. Fascinated, I tuned in more closely. When I heard, "You have to wash the kitchen floor," I looked over my shoulder, wondering who said that. Then I had a little talk with myself about the floor. "Self," I asked, "do you *choose* to clean the kitchen floor?" "Well," my Self answered, "I can't walk barefoot anymore." After my discussion, I decided that I *did want* to wash the floor. Doing it, then, wasn't half bad, because *I had chosen to do it*! That was the beginning of a long, gradual shift toward my internal locus of control.

In our culture we are externally oriented. Our possessions, appearance, performance, and what others think are all given tremendous importance. The internal—what *we* think, what *we* need, what *we* value, what gives *us* meaning in life—is often considered unimportant and ignored.

Many people think that self-esteem comes from others, from something external. They think that someone else is responsible for their happiness. The fact is: for adults, *self*-esteem is something that you give to your*self*.

Only you can give yourself self-respect.
Only you can give yourself self-acceptance.
Only you can give yourself self esteem.

Typically, people try to gain self-esteem from sources external to themselves, through

- *What they do.* Many people work very hard doing many things for others. They shift from being human beings to human doings.
- *What they have.* Many people collect material possessions. "He who dies with the most toys wins," reads a bumper sticker. They may compete with others, buy a bigger boat than the Joneses.
- *What they know.* Many people try to impress others with information and with the many books they have read.
- *How they perform.* Many people are acutely aware of how they affect others, and they operate their lives attempting to achieve a desired effect on others.
- *How they look.* Many people put a great amount of time, effort, and money into their appearance.
- *Who they are with.* Many people think that being with a "good" partner makes them okay.

The ultimate hope in each of these cases is that others will notice and approve of them; then they will be okay. Their self-esteem is based on externals. They are people-pleasers and approval-seekers who have given others the power to control their self-esteem. This "self-esteem is conditional, for example: "If I do _____, I am okay." "If I look beautiful, I am okay." "If I act _____, I am okay." Conversely, if I don't do _____, I am not okay." They strive for an illusion of self-esteem that may never occur.

These external conditional sources of self-esteem are not solid. I may feel okay today because I have a bigger boat than the Joneses; yet tomorrow they might buy an even better one. I may feel okay today because I've read every book on the best-seller list; yet next month I may not have time. Or I may feel okay because I did a thousand things for my family; yet if I stop doing all those things (possibly because of exhaustion), then I'm not okay, and my self-esteem drops.

Self-esteem is not what you do or have or know—it works from the inside out rather than from the outside in. Self-esteem is internal. Self-esteem is based on who you are. Real self-esteem is based on believing that you are lovable and worthwhile.

As you accept, respect, and cherish yourself more, you can take charge of your own self-esteem and stop working so hard to please others. By becoming more pleasing to yourself, you esteem yourself more, and you become more pleasing to others in the process. (See Chapter 18.)

Unconditional self-esteem is based on unconditional love for yourself. The First Commandment tells us to love our neighbors as ourselves. This means that we should love ourselves, then love our neighbors (and our children) as well. In reality, if I hate myself, I can't love my kids or my neighbor very well. And if I believe that I am not lovable, it's hard to imagine that my kids or anyone else might really love me—even when they do. It begins with a choice, plus a change of self-talk and a change of heart.

Positive self-esteem is the choice and commitment to respect, accept, and love yourself completely. It is the best gift you can give to yourself. Your self-esteem is in your hands.

The process of parenting begins with externally oriented little children who learn their value from significant people in their lives. We nudge them toward becoming internally oriented adults who can think for themselves, who can trust themselves, and who have internalized self-esteem.

Three specific suggestions that lead to internalization are

• Use the natural-and-logical-consequences style of discipline. This approach teaches kids to figure things out, to think for themselves, and to become *self*-disciplined. The focus on inner motivation leads to internal-locus-of-control development in the child. The reward-and-punishment approach is based on externals—force and manipulation. It results in a submissive behavioral style that thwarts the process of maturation and that creates people pleasers.

• Use more encouragement and less praise. Praise is a verbal reward that shows children that they are pleasing to adults. The danger is that children might learn to behave and perform for the purpose of pleasing others and receiving their approval. Praise supports external-locus-of-control behavior. Encouragement, on the other hand, inspires internally and motivates them *from within*. The child observes the support, knows that you believe in him or her, achieves something, and gains higher self-esteem *directly* from the experience. Encouragement leads to the development of an internal locus of control.

• Turn off the television, the radio, and the walkman. Relax! Then listen. Turn down the endless bombardment of noise and chatter. Listen! Listen to the soft inner voice. Then do what is good for you. This is equally important for your children and for yourself. Kids may complain of boredom at first. That's okay. I remember a classmate saying that the most creative and best times of her childhood came shortly after she announced that she was bored. Instead of looking for external satisfaction, she looked within and tapped her inner resources.

Someone once said that quiet time is the most important time in your life. Take long walks. Meditate. Write in a journal. Listen to your inner guidance system (not to be confused with the chatter of self-talk). Listen to your body. Learn to trust it. No one knows better than yourself what is best for you. And that still, small voice inside will reveal what that is.

We can encourage the transition from an external to an internal locus of control. As we support the developmental process in our kids, we can also support it in ourselves. We can grow and develop right alongside of them. And the more we develop ourselves, the more we have to give to our children.

Chapter Twenty

Play

"One joy scatters a hundred griefs."
—Chinese proverb

Play is a universal language. It gives a sense of joy in being alive. It is one of the healthiest things we have in our culture. When we play, we give a gift of joy to another.

Happy and joyous family times are a unifying force. They increase closeness and positive feelings. They increase loyalty to the family team. Everyone relaxes and feels more alive. Love just happens when you're having fun together!

One of the most special times I shared with my children happened right after I said, "Take me into your world." Leaving my parent-self at home, I entered the magical and mysterious world of the young. We went down the bike path to an irrigation ditch, walked cautiously over the bridge ("That's where the troll lives, Mom"), and down a crooked, narrow path. We stopped in front of a tree ("Put your feet right here, stoop down, and squint, Mom") to see the Dr. Seuss creature's face in the trunk. That little experience was great fun for all of us! It bridged the worlds of parent and child and brought us closer. And that memory will enrich me forever.

Kids are a great excuse to be silly. If you roll down a grassy hill by yourself, someone is sure to raise their eyebrows. But if you take a kid along, no one will think twice about it. If they do, it will probably be, "How wonderful to see parents playing with their children!"

Children are our natural teachers, but to learn best from them, we must meet them at their level. They can help us remember how to play—how to build forts or play leapfrog. They can encourage us to try new adventures—like riding a skateboard—and help us remember some wonderful old ones like Hide and Seek or squirt-gun fights.

Through them, we can learn to see the world differently—with curious, childlike eyes. With them we can cut loose from stuffy adultness, be totally foolish—and get away with it! We can reclaim forgotten parts of ourselves and rediscover some beautiful qualities of our childhood.

What did you love to do as a kid? Have you shared jacks and kickthe-can with your children? Some of the best times of my childhood were spent playing outdoors with my neighborhood friends. Remember the wonderful, joyous things, and do them with your kids.

To many kids with a high TV diet, play now means passively waiting to be entertained; put-downs, humiliation, and violence are presented as "humor"—and artificial laughter indicates that they are "supposed to" laugh. (See Chapter 19.) Watching TV, they don't learn about actively having fun, and they may come to believe that playing involves only the limited games and toys that Mom and Dad have to buy for them. They may know nothing about the creativity that goes into building a dam, or a treehouse. Furthermore, if they don't learn to play as a kid, they may never learn.

My oldest kids are of the generation that has grown up with television. My daughter often complains that to most people her age fun means watching TV and/or drinking beer. If the drinks are half price, it's Happy Hour. So they sit around feeding their respective addictions and wonder, "Are we having fun yet?"

Kids are born with inner joy. Play is as natural as breathing to them. For kids, there is no work-play separation until they learn dualistic thinking from the adult world: work is what you have to do and don't like, and play is what you love to do but don't have time for. Yet work can become play with an attitude shift. Having a vegetable garden, for example, can be drudgery or it can be a joy. If we put fun back into our own work, we will want to do it and our kids will be more eager to join in. Work is play until parents teach kids that it's work—then they learn to resist it.

Childhood is a time of phenomenal growth, aliveness, and delight. Growing up, for many, has meant ending this amazing process. A young man once said to me, "Growing up in America is the process of growing numb." Many have come to associate growing up with a loss of excitement and eagerness to learn. Playfulness has slowly disappeared from their lives. Yet this need not be a terminal condition. Ask a kid how to play, and you will recapture dormant parts of yourself, bringing joy and vitality back into your life.

Learning is also play; it is the joyous foundation of life. Every time we learn something new, we become someone new. If learning is forced upon kids, it becomes "work." If you play at learning, it's a delight.

Play is very important for adults. It's fun, stress reducing, and generally therapeutic. Several years ago I attended a concert—a "Kazoo-phony"—presented by musicians who claimed to have attended the Eastman Kazoovatory of Music. On kazoos, they played the 1812 Overture and "The Plight of the Kazoomblebee"! The kazoo, they said, is to classical music what a total body cast is to ballet. Those people have rediscovered their playfulness and are being financially rewarded for bringing childish joy and laughter into people's lives.

When my kids were young, I collected rhythm instruments. Periodically we would take them out of the closet, turn on some lively music, and all become musicians. Sometimes we took out hats to add to the fun and marched and paraded around the house together. (My husband and I sometimes took them out for adult parties, giving the cymbals to the most reserved person there.) Perhaps it's a coincidence that all three of my kids seem to have an excellent sense of rhythm!

Another way we would play was to the record of "Peter and the Wolf." The living room would suddenly become the meadow, and each person became a character, learning to identify with the instruments and themes. Usually we would end up playing several different parts; there was almost always an argument over who got to be the wolf. This charade was a wonderful way to spend time together.

If you aren't already involved in playing with your kids, there are a few simple hints to follow:

• Play needs to be fun for everyone. When you tease or tickle your kids, watch them; if it's not fun for them, stop doing it. Some parents toss a baby into the air, saying "What fun!" and continue even if the baby starts to cry. If your game's not working, change it. Kids may feel violated by well-meaning parents and older siblings who tease them too far.

• Play is best when everyone comes out winning. If you really want your kids to win, you will coach and cheer for them and be happy when they succeed. "New Games" are based on the belief that we don't have to make others lose in order to win. It is a noncompetitive approach to play involving team building. Tail of the Dragon, for example, involves a line of people, each holding on to the waist of the person in front of them. The last person has a kerchief hanging from his pocket—the "tail"—and the first person—the head of the dragon— has to try to catch it. There are always gales of laughter, and everyone's self-esteem goes up.

• When parents "have to" beat their kids at a game, the kids are set up to lose. This isn't play, but a power ploy with the losers being victimized. Parents are bigger, older, and smarter than kids; they can win all the time if they want. Kids who lose all the time become discouraged and don't want to play anymore because they know they will lose. Nobody likes to lose. The parent may win the game, but the relationship suffers as does the child's attitude toward play. If your parents played with you in this way, remember how it felt. Did you ever shrug and say, "It doesn't really matter," when it did? That kind of play wasn't fair—and it wasn't fun. Learn from—don't repeat—the mistakes of your parents. Give yourself permission to change. Decide to play so that both of you enjoy the experience and feel good.

• There's folk wisdom that states, "A dirty kid is a happy kid." To tell your kid, "Go out and play but don't get dirty" is a setup for disappointment. Kids often do get dirty when they're having a good time. A dirty, excited kid may be healthier than a clean, discouraged one.

Playing can develop your sense of humor—and that of your kids. A regular dose of giggles, guffaws, chortles, and chuckles does wonderful things for your emotional well-being.

Play also has a powerful influence on health. Norman Cousins refused to accept the prognosis of his chronic, debilitating disease; he refused to believe that he would only get worse, then die. He decided instead to get well—and to do anything and everything necessary to accomplish that. In his book *Anatomy of an Illness,* he describes his recovery.[1]

Accepting responsibility for his body and his illness, Cousins began to work very closely with his physician to counter the disease process. Understanding the close body-mind relationship underlying psychosomatic disease, he decided to use the full force of his mind and body to defeat this disease process. If, he concluded, we can create disease in our bodies by negative thoughts, beliefs, and attitudes, we also have the power to reverse that process and create healthy bodies instead.

He filled his hospital room with laughter and giggles. Every day he watched old Charlie Chaplin movies and laughed until his sides ached. Over time—and with lots of fun—he actually reversed the progress of his "terminal" disease!

Not only do laughter and play stimulate the immune system, they can reduce stress. Exercise is a form of play for many—running, dancing, hiking, swimming—and the people you "play" with easily become your friends.

Play increases health, happiness, and harmony. It creates bonds between people. It enhances personal growth and self-esteem. A gift that keeps giving, your play of today builds a store of rich memories for you to draw upon when you are old.

For those who don't enjoy themselves, life is a burden, others can be a burden, and they are a burden to themselves. Everyone's self-esteem tends to sag. Enjoying yourself, on the other hand, is one of the greatest things you can do for yourself. And because joy is contagious, others will also benefit.

Start to play today. Look for things that tickle your funny bone. Put down this book and do one fun thing you love to do. Right now. You deserve joy in your life! It's never too late to have a happy childhood.

Chapter Twenty-One

The Winning Environment

"If a seed is given good soil and plenty of water and sun,
it doesn't have to try to unfold.
It doesn't need self-confidence or self-discipline or perseverance.
It just unfolds. As a matter of fact, it can't help unfolding."

—Barbara Sher[1]

Human beings need optimal growing conditions in order to thrive. For those who did not have them as a child, growth and development may have been impaired. Yet seeds may lie dormant for a long time until the environment improves—the sun shines, the rain comes, a rock is moved away. Then they can grow, blossom, and bear fruit.

Remembering your family environment as a child, consider the following questions.

1. Could you trust your parents—knowing that they would take care of your needs (food, shelter, acceptance, and love) and protect you from harm?
2. Were you respected and loved just for being you?
3. Did your parents realize that you were unique and special and make you feel that way?
4. Did they believe in you and encourage you to be your best?
5. Did you feel that your ideas and opinions were taken seriously?
6. Were you encouraged to discover and explore your special talents and interests?
7. Did they encourage you to do things for yourself—including solving your own problems?
8. Did they set limits and also allow freedom?
9. Were you told that you could be and do anything you wanted? Were you given support and encouragement to do so?
10. Did you know that when you got in over your head you could turn to them for help—without reproach?[2]

If you answered yes to many of these questions, yours was probably a winning environment. If you answered with many no's, realize that your parents probably gave you more than they had received. They probably did the best they could at the most difficult and challenging job, parenting. They made mistakes, as we all do; learn from them and forgive them. Be grateful for all the good things they gave you.

We are all winners. Yet some people are disguised as losers. In their childhood environment perhaps no one saw their beauty or made them feel beautiful. Perhaps no one saw their hidden greatness and the important gifts they had for the world. Perhaps no one believed in them, supported them, or encouraged them to become winners. They became losers because they didn't know that they were really winners.

Many people who lacked important nutrients as children become late bloomers. They fill their areas of deficiency and learn new skills. They grow, blossom, and bear fruit. It's never too late to become the beautiful, healthy, and happy person you were meant to be.

Imagine how different your life would be now if you had grown up in a winning environment. Imagine what your family of today might become if you were to create a winning environment. All children have the potential for becoming winners. If they can be winners in their own families, they are on the road to a successful life.

It all begins with a decision. You can use all the tools in this book— affirming yourself and your children, finding new ways to talk and play together . . . You can make big changes a little at a time. You cannot turn back the clock. But you can begin now.

As you create a healthier environment for your children, you create if for yourself; as you create it for yourself, you create it for your children. At first it may be hard work—change is usually difficult. But it will get easier and better. Be patient. It takes time. Each little change is a movement toward becoming a Winning Family.

Chapter Twenty-Two

Extending Your Family

"The bond that links your true family is not one of blood,
but of respect and joy in each other's life."

—Richard Bach[1]

Before 1936, most American families were multigenerational extended families. They were not only the center of work, education, recreation, and worship; they also constituted economic production units. In rural settings, cooperation was necessary for survival.

Kids would see how grandparents, aunts, and uncles got along with others, how they made judgments and decisions, how they solved problems. They would get outside opinions from various people they trusted. They watched adults handle important human emotions and major life events: childbirth, sickness, and death. If a parent died, aunts and uncles could fill in to keep the family going.

Rubbing elbows with lots of relatives, children learned to get along with different types of people. Many adults shared responsibility for the children. Working side by side with others, children got direct on-the-job training for living.

I grew up in an extended family in Detroit. My German-immigrant parents met there and married shortly after. My father's brother, Franz, lived with the family for twenty years. Uncle Franz was a barber. As a child, I would sit on his lap and comb his hair. I would walk with him to visit his friends. I saw his world and how he related to it. I learned much from him. Sharing special time together, we developed a loving bond between us.

Families have changed dramatically—from the extended family, to the nuclear family, and now to an amazing diversity of family forms. Children of today grow up in a variety of family units. One in five children lives in a "blended" or stepfamily. One in four lives in a single-parent family. More than half the children under age six are cared for by a childcare provider while parents work. And there are 2 million "latchkey children" who are unsupervised during afterschool hours.

Today we have smaller households; a greater proportion have few or no children, and there are an increasing number of single-person households—families of one. Individuals are more isolated, more alone. A man I know commented that when he was growing up, neighbors would always poke their heads through the kitchen door in the morning and ask, "Is the coffee on?" Where he lives today, he is on speaking terms with the neighbors, but only to the point of making small talk about the car or the weather. The days of neighborhoods serving as community support groups are all but gone.

Every year in the United States, 40 million people move from one place to another.[2] They uproot themselves for a variety of reasons; many move great distances, leaving grandparents, friends, and neighbors behind. Some move to withdraw from the pain and problems of dysfunctional families. Some move to pursue job or educational opportunities. Transplanting their families to new settings, they must start over from the beginning—recreating important connections with others.

Within the last fifty years there have been enormous splits in families, physically and emotionally; the two often go hand in hand. For many, important natural family connections have been seriously weakened or severed.

In the case of divorce, for example, the vital grandparent-grandchild bond is frequently interrupted or damaged at a time when kids most desperately need support and stability. In the past, aunts and uncles and grandparents often filled in during times of crisis until the family recovered. Kids had someone familiar to cling to throughout the turmoil.

Divorce stems from problems between husband and wife. It should not create a major rift between two families. The kids are not divorcing a parent, nor grandparents, aunts, or uncles. They should not lose those special people at a time when they most need loving suport.

It is possible for a divorced couple to heal their wounds over time and even become friends with each other. In this healthy option, there is less pain and harm to the kids and the rest of the family. I have a friend who is on such good terms with her ex-husband (and his second wife) that she is godmother to their two children, and although they live over a thousand miles apart, they see each other at least once a year.

Mothers-in-law have inherited an undeserved cultural stereotype. Unfairly labeled "the enemy," they are the butt of many jokes that set them up for rejection, divisiveness, and pain. The same is true for stepmothers. Negative attitudes create a prejudice that may undermine those relationships and reflect in the quality of the grandparent-grand-child, stepparent-stepchild connection.

Grandparents are natural self-esteem developers, yet they often live too far away to maintain close contact with their children. The greatest of natural resources for making kids feel important may themselves be feeling unimportant, lonely, and unneeded hundreds of miles away. This loving cross-generational kinship connection has been danger-ously weakened.

Everyone needs someone to turn to when things are tough. The hard work of childrearing is lightened by having someone share laughter, a meal, a walk in the park. "Joy shared is joy doubled; sorrow shared is sorrow cut in half."

When my children were young, a fifteen-year-old boy from Georgia lived with our nuclear family for a summer. Paul did yard work for us and at times helped with the kids. We all enjoyed our "extended fam-ily" so much that we invited him back the following year. Now, despite the miles that separate us, a loving bond connects us with him. Paul is part of our family.

Later on, my daughter, Kristen, extended the family even further. Attending college in Santa Fe, she interviewed with a family looking for a baby-sitter for their three young sons. They immediately fell in love with each other. Kristen became part of their family, just as Paul had become part of ours. Moving in with them, she continued a pat-tern she had learned was acceptable and desirable in her childhood. When we visited her for the holidays, we were graciously, lovingly, and openly taken in by her adopted family.

This new variety of extended family is becoming more widespread today. Consciously or unconsciously, people are seeking out others to fill the void created by the absence of family members. Co-workers may become siblings or cousins. Neighbors may fill in as parents or grandparents. Many families are sharing their kids, spreading the re-sponsibility around a bit, creating the support they need, and enrich-ing their lives.

After creating a "surrogate family," Kathy (a workshop participant) reflected, "Our biological families contain structured roles that lock us into a track of behavior much like a roller-coaster. As we grow and change, it becomes difficult to break away from these predefined roles. The surrogate family, by contrast, begins at the point at which we left the biological one. There are few preconceived notions about us, and we're allowed to be ourselves. We can interact without the fear of criticism or comparison. We can *choose* our surrogate family mem-bers."

Many couples, with or without children, are choosing to have another person share their homes with them. The honesty and realness that happen in live-in situations can create deep bonds. There is, of course, increased possibility for friction, but there is also increased opportunity for enrichment. These roommates become part of each other's lives—even after they have separated.

In 1936 a group of twelve young mothers from a farm community in Colorado formed a social club called The Diligent Dozen so that they could go somewhere with their children and completely enjoy themselves. They had all moved west with their husbands and met monthly with each other to do mending and fancy work while their children played. Afterward they enjoyed games that had been planned by the hostess. The husbands, who affectionately called the club The Dirty Dozen were welcome if they came. They had big feasts at holidays. As original members passed away over the years, they invited new women to join. Through repeated contact, they developed a deep bond—"like family"—among themselves.[3]

People who have ongoing significant contact with children—childcare providers, baby-sitters, neighbors—are part of their extended family. They play very important roles in children's lives, in their development. As kids get older, they may seek out and "adopt" surrogate family members who can enrich their lives as well as our own.

We need many caring people in our lives. We need to come together in ways that matter, that sustain and enrich us. We can share ourselves and our children. When we extend our families, we expand our lives.

Chapter Twenty-Three

The Winning Family

"The greatest gifts you can give your children are the roots of responsibility and the wings of independence."
—Denis Waitly[1]

Winning families come in a variety of forms, sizes, and colors. They have qualities in common that contribute to a high level of self-worth in their members. The climate is comfortable; people feel "at home" in their homes.

There is a strong sense of sharing and connectedness in a family team. Members know that they are important, that they belong. Yet given the wings of independence, they are encouraged to find and create their own meaning and purpose in life and to realize their own dreams. Balancing closeness and separateness, they enjoy spending time together and apart. Individuals do their own thing and are also committed to the well-being of others, of the whole family.

Last spring, my sons created a memorable winning event. Damian (age 23) offered to be the chauffeur for Felix's senior prom. He borrowed a Mercedes-Benz from a professor, decorated the inside with silk roses, and dressed for the part. Being short on money, Felix and his friend Jeff decided to cook dinner at our home. I ironed my best tablecloth and borrowed silver candelabra and serving pieces.

The boys spent many hours shopping and cooking. Suddenly it was time to put on their tuxedos and leave. Damian chauffeured Felix to pick up his date while I picked up the pieces in the kitchen, Later, exchanging cap for apron, the chauffeur became the waiter. He served the lobster tails (which he presented as "giant roly-polys"). Felix called for the (nonalcoholic) wine. Damian dramatically opened the wired-on champagne cap and uncovered a screw-on cap, which everyone sniffed without cracking a smile. In the kitchen, I loved every minute of it! My heart was full of love and joy and delight with my winning family.

The winning family operates on the principle that *everyone* has a right to win. This team encourages and supports all its players in discovering their unique interests and talents. Through believing in, coaching, and cheering for one another, they set themselves up for success. No one has to lose.

Parents become a winning example—in an area of importance to them—and they let their own lives show the way. They want to be successful and set themselves up to do so; they model winning. They also want their spouses and kids to win and set them up to do so, too. "If I help you win, I win; if you help me win, you win." That everyone can come out winning is an underlying belief. No one, therefore, wants to win at another's expense.

To create a Winning Family, it is necessary to redefine *winning*. Winning can no longer be defined as competing with, overpowering, intimidating, and putting others down. That is the win-lose model. A new definition of winning is to be your best and do the best you can. A desire for excellence—in self and for others—is the trait of a real winner.

Winning Families are made up of high-quality relationships based on mutual respect, acceptance, honesty, trust, cooperation, loyalty, and faith in others. The parents honestly know and accept themselves, including their feelings and weaknesses. They can, therefore, accept feelings and weaknesses in each other and in their children. The win-win belief is relational; one can't be a winner without caring, sharing, and empowering others to win.

The well-being of individuals is a very high priority. Rules—as few as possible and as many as necessary—are made for the benefit of the whole family, not just the rulemaker. Rules validate and promote self-worth in individuals and harmony in the family. Parents create rules that say that human life and feelings are more important than anything else.

In winning families, people are listened to and heard. They enjoy spending time with each other. Everything is out in the open; there is no need for secrets or dishonesty. Family members are genuine with each other; they don't have to pretend or play a role. They know they are accepted and loved for who they are.

This healthy family has an openness to new people and new ideas. The whole family system is adaptable to life's changes—including new role definitions—and accepts and encourages change as a potential source of growth.

The climate is characterized by aliveness, genuineness, and love. It is okay to take risks. It is safe to be honest and real. A winning family is a high-self-esteem team.

The "Perfect Family" model that is held up to us as an ideal never has problems. Everyone is always happy, always smiling, always clean. Expectations of perfection—to be a perfect parent, a perfect husband or wife, or a perfect kid—are setups for frustration, disappointment, anger, pretense, and low self-esteem. The perfect family is a myth. It is a performance—like posing for a snapshot—that is a barrier to intimacy. It creates a great deal of stress when confused with real life.

On the other hand, the Winning Family is like a moving picture, in which things are always happening, where people are changing and growing. A winning family is always in process. Of course they have problems—everyone has problems—but they have skills to deal with them and the confidence that they will overcome them. When they need help, they have the wisdom to get it.

You can create a Winning Family—a family in which everyone feels like a success. It's very difficult to do in our win-lose culture. But it's worth the effort. There's great joy and a depth of connection that can happen when you replace old negative habits with new high-self-esteem behavior and attitudes. It all begins with a decision.

The Winning Family has nothing to do with awards or trophies. It has to do with liking, loving, and enjoying each other. It has to do with satisfaction. A Winning Family feels good.

A Winning Family begins with parents who have a high level of self-worth—the higher their own self-esteem and sense of competence, the more likely they are to create a Winning Family team. It begins with the desire for everyone to be a success within the family and with a decision to learn and apply the skills to make that happen.

Postscript:
On Nightmares

"Until now, every generation throughout history lived with the tacit certainty that other generations would follow. Each assumed, without questioning, that its children and children's children and those yet unborn would carry on—to walk the same earth, under the same sky."
—Joanna Rogers Macy[1]

As parents, we give our children the gift of life—and the necessary tools to live it well. We need to protect them from harm and give them comfort during nightmares, assuring them that they will be okay. Yet our children are growing up in a nightmare. We are all living in a nightmare.

Children, realizing that they may not have a chance to grow up, can become intensely angry. They are aware of the imminent danger of global annihilation. They feel confused, powerless, and desperate.

It's hard to work for a happy family when you think the world is going to blow up!

Never since the beginning of time has there been such danger to ourselves, our children, and our grandchildren. Toxic wastes, acid rain, rising rates of radioactivity, dying seas, loss of topsoil and forest-land, and expiring species of plants and animals are all signs of a progressive destruction of our life-support system. The air we breathe, the food we eat, the water we drink are often polluted. Parents and children alike are aware of these life-threatening realities. It's a hard time to be a kid—or a parent. It is also an exciting time—living on the edge of a breakthrough.

"No other generation has inherited this enormous responsibility and the privilege of saving all past and all future generations, all animals and all plants," states Australian pediatrician Helen Caldicott.[2] She goes on to say that rapid nuclear disarmament is the ultimate issue of parenting. It is also the ultimate issue of preventive medicine and religion.

Bringing a child into the world is the greatest act of hope there is.

It is our statement of trust that life will go on—that we will enjoy our children and our children's children. We must hope, but we can no longer take the future for granted.

We need to look at our beliefs—about war, about peace. If we believe that war is inevitable, we develop a victim mentality, saying to ourselves, "My life is at the mercy of forces beyond my control. There's nothing I can do." In thinking this way, we disempower ourselves. We do nothing. Nothing changes. We feel afraid and desperate.

If, on the other hand, we choose to believe that peace is possible—and that it is our responsibility—it's very different. We tell ourselves, "I can make a difference. I know I can. If it's to be, it's up to me." We look for opportunities to become involved. We empower ourselves to take action. We feel hopeful. We act and things change. Even if our contributions are small, they can make a big difference.

In understanding the qualities of winning families—respect, responsibility, caring, seeing cause-and-effect relationships, fixing mistakes and learning from them, believing that it's unethical to "win" while damaging others—we understand some principles for winning communities and for a winning world.

We must hold ourselves and our children accountable—and also our political leaders. Let us remind them that our American democracy was founded on a government of the people, by the people, and for the people—of present and future generations. Let us accept our responsibility and challenge to make the world truly safe for our children. Let us act on the belief that what we do will make a difference.

We must begin where we are. We must do what we can. The first step to bringing peace to the world is to bring it to yourself and your family.

A peaceful world is the best setting for A Winning Family.

Resources Available to Parents

Often during the years of parenting, I felt very isolated. I did not know how to make friends, or how to be a friend. (Talking only about husbands and kids as I'd learned to do is not a basis for friendship.) At that time, I also did not appreciate the importance of friendships, especially when relatives are distant. I was not aware that it was my responsibility to find and create supports. I now know that I am responsible for developing the self-support, people-support, and system-support that I need.

Though I felt isolated, I was, in fact, not alone. There were thousands of people around me, but I didn't have the self-confidence, assertiveness, or people-skills to ask for what I needed. My hope, in writing this book, is to teach those skills and encourage you to reach out to others—for friendship, for fun, for support.

- Many churches are family oriented and very supportive. If yours is not, express your needs. Ask first for what you want. Your needs are not yours alone but are shared by others.
- Many communities have parenting centers that offer education and support to moms and dads.
- Classes and workshops are offered through community agencies.
- Agencies such as United Way sponsor supportive programs in various communities. For example, the Respite Center in Madison, Wisconsin, is available for those times "when the kids, the house, the job are all closing in . . . and a break would do a world of good."

If you have difficulty locating help, your county mental health center should have information on local resources.

You are not alone. Friendships, support, educational programs, and counseling are available. Remember, whatever you're looking for you'll find.

If you feel overwhelmed at times, don't panic. Figure out what you. need, then ask for it or go and get it. Sometimes what you need is to get away from the kids for a while—walk in the woods, visit a friend— to help you regain perspective. Take good care of yourself, for your own sake *and* for theirs.

Recommended Reading

Black, Claudia. *It Will Never Happen To Me.* (Denver, Col.: M.A.C. Publishers, 1982).

Blanchard, Kenneth, and Spencer Johnson. *The One-Minute Manager.* (New York: Berkeley Books, 1981).

Briggs, Dorothy Corkille. *Your Child's Self-Esteem.* (New York: Doubleday, 1970).

Clarke, Jean Illsley. *Self-Esteem: A Family Affair.* (Minneapolis, Minn.: Winston Press, 1978).

Clarke, Jean Illsley. *Help! For Parents and Children.* (a series of books covering developmental stages from birth to 19 years). (New York: Harper & Row, 1986).

Dinkmeyer, Donald, and Gary D. McKay. *The Parent's Handbook: Systematic Training for Effective Parenting.* (Circle Pines, Minn.: American Guidance Service, 1982).

Dyer, Wayne. *Your Erroneous Zones.* (New York: Avon Publishers, 1977).

Palmer, Patricia. *Liking Myself.* (San Luis Obispo, Calif.: Impact Publishers, 1977).

Palmer, Patricia. *The Mouse, the Monster, and Me.* (San Luis Obispo, Calif.: Impact Publishers, 1977).

Sher, Barbara. *Wishcraft: How to Get What You Really Want.* (New York: Viking, 1979).

Smedes, Lewis B. *Forgive and Forget.* (New York: Pocket Books, 1984).

About Author

Louise Hart conducts training seminars for conferences, businesses, schools, and churches around the country. Also, an audio cassette tape program entitled *The Winning Family* is available. For further information write to:

Louise Hart
P.O. Box 7495
Boulder, Colorado 80306

Notes

Epigraph

1. Leo F. Buscaglia, *Living, Loving and Learning* (Ballantine Books). p. 262. 1983. Used by permission of the author

Chapter One

1. From the author's workshop brochure "Building Self-Esteem in Children."

Chapter Two

1. Henry David Thoreau, quoted in *2,715 One-Liner Quotations for Speakers, Writers and Raconteurs* by Edward F. Murphy (New York: Crown Publishers, 1981).
2. Eleanor Roosevelt, *This is My Story*, 1937
3. Affirmation from Jack Canfield tapes, *Self-Esteem: The Key to Success*, a six-cassette album available from Self-Esteem Seminars, 17156 Palisades Circle, Pacific Palisades, CA 90272

Chapter Three

1. Eric Hoffer, quoted in *Bits and Pieces* (Fairfield, N.J.: Economics Press, September 1986), p. 17.
2. Samual Osherson, "Finding our Fathers," *Utne Reader* (April/May 1986), PP. 36–41.
3. Mildred Newman, Bernard Berkowitz, with Jean Owen, *How to be Your Own Best Friend* (New York: Random House, 1973)
4. Leo F. Buscaglia, *Living, Loving and Learning*, Slack, Inc. 1982, used by permission.

Chapter Four

1. John Powell, *The Secret of Staying in Love* (Allen, Tex.: Argus Communications, 1974).

2. Julie Rigg and Julie Copeland, *Coming Out! Women's Voices, Women's Lives* (Melbourne N.S.W., Australia: Nelson Press, 1985).
3. Parent Effectiveness Training teaches listening skills based on Rogerian counseling principles.
4. Leo F. Buscaglia, *Loving Each Other* (Thorofare, N.J.: Slack, 1984).

Chapter Five

1. Virginia Mae Axline, *Dibs: In Search of Self* (Boston, Mass.: Houghton Mifflin, 1964).
2. Concepts adapted from Patricia Palmer, *The Mouse, the Monster and Me* (San Luis Obispo, Calif.: Impact Publishers, 1977).
3. "Saying 'no' means . . ." and the value of "no" . . . exercise from Claudia Black.

Chapter Six

1. Anne Morrow Lindbergh, quoted in Murphy, loc. cit.
2. Dorothy Corkille Briggs, *Building Self-Esteem in Children* (Garden City, N.Y.: Doubleday and Co., Dolphin Books, 1975), pp. 98, 101.
3. Claudia Black, *It Will Never Happen to Me* (Denver, Col.: M.A.C. Publications, 1982), p. 42.
4. T. Gordon, *Parent Effectiveness Training* (New York: Wyden, 1973), p. 13.
5. Leander Kech, *A Future for a Historical Jesus,* Philadelphia: Fortune Press, 1980.
6. Briggs, loc. cit., pp. 73, 74.
7. Quoted in Murphy, loc. cit.
8. Concepts adapted from Nathaniel Branden tape.
9. Buscaglia, *Loving Each Other,* loc. cit., p. 154.
10. Concept from Jack Canfield tapes, loc. cit.
11. Lewis B. Smedes, *Forgive and Forget* (New York: Pocket Books, 1984).
12. Ibid.
13. Clyde Reid, *Celebrate the Temporary* (New York: Harper and Row, 1972).

Chapter Seven

1. Henry Wadsworth Longfellow, "Table Talk," *Driftwood,* 1857.
2. Concepts adapted from Jean Illsley-Clarke, *Self-Esteem: A Family Affair* (Minneapolis, Minn.: Winston Press, 1978).
3. Ibid.
4. T. Gordon, loc. cit., p. 45.

Chapter Eight

1. Quoted in Robert Ricker, *Love Me When I'm Most Unlovable (Reston, Va.: National Association of Secondary School Principals.*
2. *Concepts adapted from Illsley Clarke, loc. cit.*

Chapter Ten

1. Marilyn French, *Beyond Power—On Women, Men, and Morals* (New York: Ballantine Books, 1985).

Chapter Eleven

1. From a cartoon by Ashleigh Brilliant, copyright 1982, Santa Barbara CA: Pot-Shots #2369.
2. Concepts adapted from Donald Dinkmeyer and Gary D. McKay, *The Parent's Handbook: Systematic Training for Effective Parenting* (Circle Pines, Minn.: American Guidance Service, 1982).
3. Bruno Betteheim, "Punishment versus Discipline," *The Atlantic* 256 (November 1985), p. 52.
4. H. S. Glenn and B. J. Wagner, *Developing Capable People.* Instructor's Manual, privately printed, undated.
5. Kenneth Blanchard and Spencer Johnson, *The One-Minute Manager* (New York: Berkley Books, 1981).

Chapter Twelve

1. *USA Today,* September 11, 1986, p. 1.
2. *USA Today,* January 21, 1985, p. 1.

Chapter Thirteen

1. Jo Coudert, *Advice from a Failure* (New York: Stein and Day Publishers, Briarcliff Manor, 1965).
2. Jesse Jackson, from a speech to the Denver Public Schools PUSH/Excel Program, August, 1979.

Chapter Fourteen

1. Statement made by my son, Felix, at age thirteen.
2. J. W. Prescott, "Body pleasure and the origins of violence," *The Futurist* (April 1975), pp. 63–74.
3. Jules Older, "A restoring touch for abusing families," *The International Journal of Child Abuse and Neglect* 5 (1981) Exercise devised by occupational therapist Franceska Banga.

4. Exercise adapted by Martha Belknap.
5. Quoted in William L. Shirer, *The Rise and Fall of the Third Reich* (New York: Simon and Schuster, 1960).
6. Linda Tschirhart Sanford, *The Silent Children* (Garden City, N.Y.: Anchor Press/Doubleday, 1980).
7. Brandt F. Steel, quoted in *St. Louis Post-Dispatch,* August 8, 1982.
8. *A Course in Miracles* (Tiburon, Calif.: Foundation for Inner Peace, 1975).

Chapter Fifteen

1. Henry Ford, quoted by Louis Tice in audiotape "New Age Thinking for Achieving Your Potential" (Seattle, Wash.: Pacific Institute).
2. Reasonable attempts to identify author have been unsuccessful.

Chapter Seventeen

1. David D. Burns, *Feeling Good: The New Mood Therapy* (New York: William Morrow, 1980), pp. 309, 310.
2. John Powell, loc. cit., p. 101.

Chapter Eighteen

1. Gloria Steinem, "A New Egalitarian Life Style," *The New York Times,* August 26, 1971.
2. Jane Fonda, *New Workout and Weight-Loss Program* (New York: Simon & Schuster, 1986).
3. Marilyn Ferguson, *The Aquarian Conspiracy: Personal and Social Transformation in the 80s* (Los Angeles: J. P. Tarcher, 1976).
4. Concepts adapted from Matthew McKay, Martha Davis, and Patrick Fanning, *The Art of Cognitive Stress Intervention* (Richmond, Calif.: New Harbinger Publications, 1981).
5. Unpublished poem by the author.

Chapter Nineteen

1. e. e. Cummings, quoted in Charles Norman, *The Magic-Maker* (New York: Macmillan, 1958).
2. Ferguson, loc. cit.

Chapter Twenty

1. Norman Cousins, *Anatomy of an Illness* (New York: Norton, 1979).

Chapter Twenty-One

1. Barbara Sher, *Wishcraft: How to Get What You Really Want* (New York: Viking, 1979).
2. Adapted from Sher, loc. cit.

Chapter Twenty-Two

1. Richard Bach, *Illusions* (New York: Delacorte, 1977).
2. United States Current Population Reports, *Geographical Mobility,* March 1983–March 1984. Series P20 #407. (Washington, D.C.: U.S. Department of Commerce, Bureau of the Census).
3. *The Greeley* [Col.] *Tribune,* January 11, 1978, and information from an interview with Bessie Cohea, 1982.

Chapter Twenty-Three

1. Quotation on a patchwork quilt expanded by Denis Waitly.

Postscript

1. Joanna Rogers Macy, *Despair and Personal Power in the Nuclear Age* (Philadelphia, Pa: New Society Publishers, 1983).
2. Helen Caldicott, "Blessed Are the Peacemakers" calendar (Berkeley, Calif.: Golden Turtle Press, 1986).

Index